DAILY DHARMA

REFLECTIONS

—— FOR ——

ADDICTION RECOVERY

First Words

Recovery is a journey that requires patience, persistence, and self-compassion. Every step forward is a victory, no matter how small it may seem. This book, offer guidance, insight, and support for those on the path of healing and self-discovery.

Daily reflection lies at the heart of Buddhist practice. Through mindful awareness, we come to understand the impermanence of our struggles, the nature of our attachments, and the boundless potential for growth. This book invites you to pause each day, to breathe, to reflect, and to take things one day at a time.

Each reflection is designed to meet you where you are, providing a theme to carry into your day. Organized in a thoughtful, structured format, this book offers guidance for practicing the Dharma and embracing the path of recovery, whether you are new to this journey or have walked it for years. The reflections are not meant to be instructional but rather contemplative and introspective—thoughts to consider as you continue your journey of healing.

Let these reflections serve as a companion on your path. As you read through each page, allow the words to inspire a deeper connection to yourself, your recovery, and the wisdom of the present moment. Whether in times of difficulty or peace, remember that the strength to heal already resides within you. All that is needed is to open your heart and mind to the process.

This book is not about achieving perfection but embracing progress. Take these reflections one day at a time, and trust that each day brings you closer to greater awareness, freedom, and peace.

JANUARY

January 1
New Horizons

"As the new year unfolds, imagine it as a blank canvas, filled with potential and possibilities. Each day is an opportunity to start fresh, to paint new experiences, and to embrace the unknown with curiosity. How does this new beginning feel to you? Perhaps it's exhilarating, or maybe it's daunting. Either way, it's a chance to set aside the past and step into the present with renewed energy."

"Reflect on the potential that lies ahead. What are you hoping to achieve or explore this year? Set aside any fears or doubts about the future. Embrace the idea that you can shape this year with your intentions and actions. It's not about having everything figured out right now; it's about being open to the journey and allowing yourself to grow."

"Take a moment to appreciate this fresh start. Breathe deeply and let go of any lingering regrets from the past. This new horizon is a gift—one that invites you to be present and engaged in the possibilities. How can you make the most of this opportunity to create something meaningful in your life today?"

January 2
Setting Intentions

"Setting intentions is like planting seeds in a garden. What you plant today will grow and shape your future. Intentions guide your actions and focus your energy. What are your intentions for this year? Are there specific goals or values you want to cultivate? Take some time to reflect on what matters most to you and how you want to align your daily actions with these intentions."

"Consider the difference between intentions and resolutions. Resolutions might feel like demands or obligations, but intentions are more about aligning your heart with your actions. What feels authentic to you? What inspires you to act with purpose? Write down your intentions and revisit them regularly to keep your focus and motivation strong."

"Remember, setting intentions isn't about perfection; it's about direction. As you move through the year, let your intentions guide you, but also allow for flexibility and growth. Life is unpredictable, and your intentions can evolve. Embrace the journey with an open heart and a willingness to adapt."

January 3
Letting Go of the Past

"The past is a collection of moments that have already passed, yet we often carry its weight with us into the present. What would it be like to let go of the burdens of yesterday? Imagine setting down the emotional baggage you've been carrying—guilt, regret, old wounds. Letting go doesn't mean forgetting; it means freeing yourself from the grip of what once was."

"Think about what you're holding onto. Is it a past mistake, a hurtful memory, or an unfulfilled expectation? Acknowledge these feelings, but also recognize that they do not define your present. Allow yourself to release them gently, without judgment. The space you create by letting go can be filled with new opportunities and fresh perspectives."

"As you move through today, practice releasing what no longer serves you. When you catch yourself dwelling on the past, gently redirect your focus to the present moment. Letting go is a process, not a one-time event. Be patient with yourself and honor the steps you take towards emotional freedom."

January
Starting Anew

"Starting anew can feel like stepping onto a fresh path, free from the footprints of the past. It's an opportunity to redefine yourself and your goals. How do you want this new beginning to look? What changes are you ready to make? Starting anew isn't about erasing the past but about building on it with a renewed sense of purpose and direction."

"Reflect on the possibilities that this new start brings. What new habits or practices would you like to incorporate into your life? What old patterns are you ready to leave behind? Embrace this moment as a chance to reinvent yourself and to pursue your goals with fresh enthusiasm."

"Starting anew is also about embracing uncertainty with courage. It's okay not to have all the answers right away. What matters is taking the first step with faith and openness. As you embark on this new chapter, be kind to yourself and recognize the strength it takes to begin again."

January 5
Acceptance

"Acceptance is about meeting reality as it is, without resistance. It's easy to wish for things to be different or to fight against circumstances we can't control. But what if today, you practiced accepting things just as they are? Acceptance doesn't mean giving up; it means recognizing and embracing the present moment with compassion."

"Consider what you're struggling to accept in your life right now. Are there situations, people, or outcomes you're fighting against? Acknowledge these struggles without judgment, and gently shift your focus to acceptance. Accepting doesn't mean liking or agreeing with everything; it means finding peace in what is."

"As you practice acceptance, you might notice a shift in your perspective. By releasing the need to control or change everything, you create space for peace and clarity. Today, focus on accepting one thing you've been resisting, and observe how this shift affects your inner state."

January 6
Forgiving Yourself

"Forgiving yourself can be one of the hardest yet most liberating acts you can perform. We often hold ourselves to high standards and carry the weight of our own mistakes and shortcomings. What if you allowed yourself to forgive those mistakes and move forward with a lighter heart? Self-forgiveness isn't about condoning past actions; it's about freeing yourself from the burden of guilt."

"Reflect on any self-blame or regret you're holding onto. What are you struggling to forgive yourself for? Recognize that everyone makes mistakes and that these do not define your worth. Embrace the idea that you are deserving of compassion and understanding, both from others and from yourself."

"As you work on forgiving yourself, remind yourself that growth comes from acknowledging and learning from mistakes, not from punishing yourself. Offer yourself kindness and patience, and take steps towards healing. Self-forgiveness is a gift you give to yourself, opening the door to a more compassionate and fulfilling life."

January 7
The Power of Now

"The present moment is where life truly happens. We often get caught up in regrets about the past or anxieties about the future, but the only moment we truly have is now. How can you bring yourself fully into the present? The power of now lies in its simplicity and immediacy. It's about being fully engaged with what's happening right now."

"Take a moment to notice your surroundings. What do you hear, see, and feel in this very moment? Practice grounding yourself in the present by focusing on these sensations. Allow yourself to experience the richness of the present without being distracted by past or future concerns."

"Embracing the power of now can bring a sense of calm and clarity. When you find yourself drifting into thoughts of what was or what might be, gently redirect your attention back to the present. This practice of mindfulness helps you connect more deeply with your life as it unfolds right now."

January 8
Finding Balance

"Finding balance is about harmonizing various aspects of your life—work, relationships, self-care, and personal growth. It's easy to become overwhelmed when one area demands too much of your attention. How can you create a sense of equilibrium in your life? Balance isn't about perfection; it's about finding a rhythm that feels right for you."

"Reflect on areas of your life that may be out of balance. Are you giving too much to one aspect while neglecting others? Consider small adjustments you can make to bring more balance into your daily routine. Balance involves both effort and ease—working towards your goals while also allowing yourself time to rest and recharge."

"As you seek balance, remember that it's a dynamic process. What feels balanced today might need adjustment tomorrow. Be open to making changes as needed and listen to your own needs and limits. Striving for balance is an ongoing journey, not a fixed destination."

January 9
Courage to Change

"Change can be daunting, but it's also an essential part of growth. The courage to embrace change is about facing the unknown with an open heart. What changes are you contemplating right now? Are there fears or uncertainties holding you back? Courage isn't the absence of fear but the willingness to move forward despite it."

"Consider what change you're resisting and why. Is it fear of failure, discomfort, or uncertainty? Acknowledge these feelings without letting them control you. Embracing change requires stepping out of your comfort zone and trusting in your ability to navigate new challenges. Each step forward, no matter how small, is a testament to your bravery."

"As you face changes, remind yourself that growth often comes from stepping into the unfamiliar. Trust yourself and your journey, and embrace the opportunities that change brings. With each act of courage, you build resilience and open the door to new possibilities."

January 10

Embracing Uncertainty

"Uncertainty is a natural part of life. We often seek to predict and control the future, but uncertainty invites us to let go of that need and trust in the process. How do you feel about uncertainty? It can be unsettling, but it also offers a space for creativity and growth. Embracing uncertainty means accepting that some things are beyond our control and finding peace in that acceptance."

"Reflect on areas of your life where uncertainty is present. What fears or worries arise when you think about the unknown? Consider how you can shift your perspective from fear to curiosity. Embracing uncertainty involves acknowledging your fears but not letting them dictate your actions. It's about finding comfort in the ambiguity of life and trusting that you can handle whatever comes your way."

"As you navigate uncertainty, practice staying present and focusing on what you can control. Embrace the possibility that uncertainty can lead to new opportunities and growth. Trust in your ability to adapt and thrive, even when the path ahead isn't clear."

January 11
Self-Compassion

"Self-compassion is about treating yourself with the same kindness and understanding that you would offer a friend. It's easy to be harsh on yourself when things don't go as planned, but self-compassion invites you to embrace yourself with warmth and care. What would it be like to extend this gentleness to yourself today? Consider moments where you might have been self-critical and reframe them with compassion."

"Reflect on ways you can show yourself kindness. Are there specific areas where you struggle to be compassionate towards yourself? Acknowledge these areas and gently remind yourself that you are worthy of love and understanding, regardless of your mistakes or shortcomings. Self-compassion allows you to recover more quickly from setbacks and fosters a more supportive relationship with yourself."

"As you practice self-compassion, notice how it influences your interactions with others. When you treat yourself with kindness, you're more likely to extend that same kindness to those around you. Embrace this practice as a way to nurture both your inner well-being and your external relationships."

January 12
Building Resilience

"Resilience is the ability to bounce back from challenges and setbacks with strength and flexibility. It's about adapting to difficulties and emerging stronger. What challenges have you faced recently? How have they tested your resilience? Building resilience involves cultivating a positive mindset and developing coping strategies to handle adversity."

"Reflect on the ways you've demonstrated resilience in the past. What strategies or attitudes helped you through tough times? Consider how you can apply these lessons to current or future challenges. Resilience is not just about enduring hardships but also about growing from them and maintaining hope."

"As you work on building resilience, focus on developing habits that support your mental and emotional strength. This might include practicing mindfulness, seeking support from others, or setting realistic goals. Embrace resilience as a continuous journey of growth and adaptation."

January 13
Setting Boundaries

"Setting boundaries is essential for maintaining your well-being and creating a healthy balance in your life. Boundaries help you protect your time, energy, and emotions. What boundaries do you need to set in your life? Reflect on areas where you might be overextending yourself or where your needs are not being met."

"Consider how you can communicate your boundaries clearly and assertively. Boundaries are not about shutting others out but about creating space for yourself to thrive. Setting boundaries involves being honest about your limits and making choices that support your well-being."

"As you establish and maintain boundaries, be mindful of how they impact your relationships and overall sense of balance. Boundaries help you honor your needs and respect yourself, fostering healthier and more fulfilling connections with others."

January 14
Letting Go of Control

"The desire to control outcomes can create stress and frustration. Letting go of control involves accepting that some things are beyond your influence and finding peace in that acceptance. What are you trying to control right now? How does this desire impact your well-being?"

"Reflect on the benefits of releasing control. When you let go of the need to micromanage every detail, you create space for spontaneity and trust. Embracing uncertainty and allowing things to unfold naturally can lead to unexpected and positive outcomes."

"Practice letting go by focusing on what you can control—your reactions and attitudes. Trust in the process and have faith that things will work out as they are meant to. Embrace the freedom that comes with surrendering control and opening yourself to new possibilities."

January 15
Fresh Beginnings

"Each day offers a chance for a fresh beginning. It's an opportunity to start over, to make different choices, and to approach life with renewed energy. What new beginnings are you considering? How can you embrace today as a chance to create something positive in your life?"

"Reflect on the potential that each new beginning holds. Whether it's a new project, a personal goal, or a shift in perspective, starting fresh can invigorate your sense of purpose and motivation. Allow yourself to let go of past constraints and approach today with a sense of optimism and possibility."

"As you embrace new beginnings, remember that every moment is a chance to begin anew. Approach each day with an open heart and a willingness to explore new opportunities. Celebrate the courage it takes to start over and honor the journey of growth and discovery."

January 16
Cultivating Patience

"Patience is the ability to remain calm and composed even when things aren't progressing as quickly as you'd like. It's about trusting the process and allowing things to unfold in their own time. What situations in your life require more patience right now? How can you practice patience in these areas?"

"Reflect on the benefits of cultivating patience. Patience helps you manage stress, build resilience, and develop a deeper understanding of yourself and others. By practicing patience, you can navigate challenges with greater ease and maintain a more balanced perspective."

"As you work on cultivating patience, focus on staying present and managing your expectations. Remind yourself that progress takes time and that every step forward is valuable. Embrace patience as a practice that enhances your well-being and enriches your life experience."

January 17
Embracing Change

"Change is a constant and inevitable part of life. Embracing change involves accepting that nothing stays the same and finding ways to adapt and thrive a midst transitions. What changes are occurring in your life right now? How can you approach these changes with openness and flexibility?"

"Reflect on your attitude towards change. Are there areas where you're resisting or struggling with transition? Consider how you can shift your perspective to see change as an opportunity for growth and learning. Embracing change involves letting go of resistance and finding ways to adapt with grace."

"As you navigate change, focus on the opportunities it brings rather than the challenges it presents. Trust in your ability to adapt and grow, and recognize that each change contributes to your overall journey. Embrace change as a natural and valuable part of life."

January 18
Mindful Reflection

"Mindful reflection involves taking time to pause, observe, and understand your thoughts and feelings. It's about being present with yourself and gaining insight into your inner world. How can you incorporate mindful reflection into your daily routine? What insights might you uncover through this practice?"

"Reflect on the importance of mindfulness in understanding yourself. Mindful reflection helps you connect with your true self and gain clarity on your emotions and motivations. By observing your thoughts and feelings without judgment, you can develop a deeper awareness of your inner experiences."

"As you practice mindful reflection, be patient with yourself and approach each session with curiosity and openness. Use this practice to gain insights into your patterns and behaviors, and to cultivate a greater sense of self-awareness and understanding."

January 19
Practicing Gratitude

"Gratitude involves recognizing and appreciating the positive aspects of your life. It's about focusing on what you have rather than what you lack. What are you grateful for today? How can practicing gratitude enhance your overall well-being and perspective?"

"Reflect on the benefits of cultivating a gratitude practice. Gratitude helps shift your focus from problems to blessings, fostering a more positive and optimistic outlook. By regularly acknowledging what you're thankful for, you can enhance your sense of contentment and joy."

"As you practice gratitude, consider keeping a gratitude journal or taking a moment each day to reflect on what you appreciate. Embrace the power of gratitude to transform your mindset and enrich your life experience. Celebrate the small and big things that bring you joy and fulfillment."

January 20
Renewed Focus

"Renewed focus involves refocusing your attention on what truly matters to you. It's about realigning your priorities and dedicating your energy to your goals and values. What areas of your life need renewed focus? How can you adjust your actions to better align with your intentions?"

"Reflect on the importance of focus in achieving your goals. Renewing your focus helps you stay motivated and make meaningful progress. Consider how you can eliminate distractions and set clear, actionable steps towards your objectives. A renewed focus enables you to channel your energy effectively and make strides toward your aspirations."

"As you work on renewing your focus, create a plan that outlines your priorities and goals. Regularly reassess your progress and make adjustments as needed. Embrace the clarity and purpose that comes with a focused mindset, and celebrate the achievements you make along the way."

January 21
Positive Affirmations

"Positive affirmations are statements that reinforce your beliefs and intentions. They help build confidence and foster a positive mindset. What positive affirmations resonate with you right now? How can incorporating affirmations into your daily routine support your growth and well-being?"

"Reflect on the power of affirmations to shape your thoughts and actions. Positive affirmations help counteract negative self-talk and reinforce your goals. By regularly repeating affirmations, you can cultivate a more optimistic and empowered outlook on life."

"As you practice positive affirmations, choose statements that are meaningful and relevant to your current journey. Repeat them with intention and belief, and observe how they influence your mindset and behavior. Embrace the transformative potential of affirmations to support your personal growth and success."

January 22
Letting Go of Perfection

"Letting go of perfection involves accepting that things don't have to be flawless to be valuable or meaningful. It's about embracing imperfections and focusing on progress rather than perfection. What areas of your life are you striving to perfect? How can you shift your perspective to appreciate the beauty in imperfection?"

"Reflect on the pressures of perfectionism and its impact on your well-being. Letting go of the need for perfection allows you to experience greater freedom and satisfaction. Embrace the idea that growth and success are not defined by perfection but by your efforts and resilience."

"As you let go of perfection, focus on celebrating your achievements and learning from your experiences. Appreciate the journey and the progress you make, rather than fixating on unattainable ideals. Embrace the imperfectly beautiful nature of your life and work."

January 23
Embracing Forgiveness

"Forgiveness involves letting go of grudges and resentment, both towards yourself and others. It's about freeing yourself from the burden of past hurts and moving forward with a lighter heart. Who do you need to forgive, including yourself? How can embracing forgiveness contribute to your healing and peace?"

"Reflect on the benefits of forgiveness in your life. Holding onto anger and resentment can hinder your emotional well-being and recovery. Forgiveness is a gift you give yourself, allowing you to release negative emotions and cultivate a more peaceful and positive mindset."

"As you practice forgiveness, approach it with an open heart and a willingness to let go. Recognize that forgiveness is a process and may take time. Embrace forgiveness as a means to enhance your emotional freedom and to build healthier and more harmonious relationships."

January 24

Exploring New Perspectives

"Exploring new perspectives involves looking at situations from different angles and being open to alternative viewpoints. It's about expanding your understanding and challenging your assumptions. What new perspectives can you explore today? How can they enrich your experience and decision-making?"

"Reflect on the value of considering different viewpoints. Exploring new perspectives can lead to greater empathy, creativity, and problem-solving. By stepping outside your usual frame of reference, you open yourself to new ideas and possibilities."

"As you explore new perspectives, approach each situation with curiosity and openness. Embrace the opportunity to learn from others and to broaden your understanding. Celebrate the growth that comes from seeing things in a new light and integrating diverse viewpoints into your life."

January 25
Nurturing Relationships

"Nurturing relationships involves investing time and energy into building and maintaining meaningful connections with others. It's about fostering trust, understanding, and mutual support. Which relationships in your life need nurturing right now? How can you show up for others and strengthen your connections?"

"Reflect on the importance of nurturing relationships in your recovery and overall well-being. Strong, supportive relationships contribute to your emotional health and provide a sense of community and belonging. Consider ways to deepen your connections and express appreciation for the people in your life."

"As you focus on nurturing relationships, prioritize open communication, empathy, and acts of kindness. Make an effort to be present and supportive, and celebrate the positive impact that strong relationships have on your life. Embrace the joy and fulfillment that comes from meaningful connections."

January 26
Embracing Vulnerability

"Embracing vulnerability involves allowing yourself to be open and honest about your emotions and experiences. It's about letting go of the fear of judgment and showing your true self. What aspects of your life do you feel vulnerable about? How can embracing vulnerability contribute to your growth and connections with others?"

"Reflect on the power of vulnerability in building authentic relationships and fostering self-acceptance. Vulnerability allows you to connect with others on a deeper level and to experience greater emotional intimacy. By embracing vulnerability, you open yourself to greater trust and support."

"As you practice embracing vulnerability, be gentle with yourself and take small steps towards openness. Recognize that vulnerability is a strength, not a weakness, and that it enhances your capacity for genuine connection and personal growth."

January 27
Cultivating Joy

"Cultivating joy involves intentionally seeking out and celebrating moments of happiness and contentment. It's about finding delight in everyday experiences and nurturing a positive outlook. What brings you joy today? How can you actively cultivate more joy in your life?"

"Reflect on the sources of joy in your life and how you can make time for them. Joy is not just a fleeting emotion but a state of mind that can be nurtured through mindful appreciation and gratitude. Embrace the small and big things that bring you happiness and satisfaction."

"As you focus on cultivating joy, create opportunities for joyfulness in your daily routine. Engage in activities that uplift your spirit and surround yourself with positive influences. Celebrate the moments of joy and let them enhance your overall well-being and resilience."

January 28
Practicing Mindful Listening

"Practicing mindful listening involves fully attending to others without distraction or judgment. It's about being present and attentive in your interactions, allowing others to feel heard and understood. How can you practice mindful listening in your conversations today? What impact might it have on your relationships?"

"Reflect on the importance of mindful listening in building meaningful connections. By actively listening, you show respect and empathy, which strengthens your relationships and fosters a deeper understanding of others. Mindful listening also helps you better respond to others' needs and concerns."

"As you practice mindful listening, focus on being present and avoiding interruptions. Give your full attention to the speaker and respond thoughtfully. Embrace the benefits of mindful listening in enhancing your communication and building stronger, more supportive relationships."

January 29
Finding Balance

"Finding balance involves harmonizing different aspects of your life to achieve a sense of equilibrium and well-being. It's about managing your time, energy, and priorities in a way that supports your overall health and happiness. Where do you feel out of balance right now? How can you adjust your approach to restore balance?"

"Reflect on the elements of your life that contribute to your sense of balance. Finding balance requires ongoing adjustments and self-awareness. Consider how you can create a more harmonious life by addressing areas where you might be overextending yourself or neglecting important aspects of your well-being."

"As you work on finding balance, prioritize activities and practices that support your health and happiness. Set realistic goals and boundaries to help you maintain equilibrium. Embrace the journey of balancing different aspects of your life and celebrate the progress you make along the way."

January 30
Embracing Self-Growth

"Embracing self-growth involves continuously striving to develop and improve yourself. It's about being open to learning, evolving, and expanding your horizons. What areas of self-growth are you focusing on right now? How can you nurture your personal development and celebrate your progress?"

"Reflect on the journey of self-growth and the steps you're taking towards personal development. Self-growth requires self-awareness, effort, and a willingness to embrace change. Consider how you can support your growth by setting goals, seeking new experiences, and reflecting on your achievements."

"As you embrace self-growth, recognize the value of every step you take towards becoming the best version of yourself. Celebrate your progress and continue to set intentions for your personal development. Embrace self-growth as an ongoing journey that enriches your life and enhances your well-being."

January 31
Embracing Inner Peace

"Embracing inner peace involves cultivating a sense of calm and tranquility within yourself. It's about finding stillness amidst the chaos and nurturing a peaceful mindset. What practices help you find inner peace? How can you integrate these practices into your daily routine?"

"Reflect on the importance of inner peace for your overall well-being. Inner peace allows you to respond to challenges with greater clarity and resilience. Consider how mindfulness, meditation, or other practices contribute to your sense of calm and stability."

"As you focus on embracing inner peace, create a space for relaxation and reflection in your daily life. Prioritize activities that nurture your sense of tranquility and reduce stress. Celebrate the moments of peace you experience and let them guide you towards a more balanced and harmonious life."

FEBRUARY

February 1
Embracing Change

"Change is a constant companion on the path of recovery. Today, take a moment to reflect on a recent change you've experienced. How did you initially react to it, and how has your perception shifted over time? Change often feels unsettling, but it can also be a powerful catalyst for growth and transformation."

"Consider the moments when change brought unexpected lessons into your life. Reflect on how these lessons have shaped your approach to recovery. Each change, no matter how small, contributes to the mosaic of your journey, guiding you towards new understanding and personal evolution."

"Approach today with an open heart, welcoming the changes that come your way. Embrace the fluidity of your path and recognize that change, though sometimes challenging, is an integral part of your growth. Allow each new experience to add depth and richness to your journey."

February 2
The Power of Acceptance

"Acceptance is not about resignation; it's about finding peace in the present moment. Reflect on a situation where acceptance was challenging for you. What thoughts and emotions arose, and how did you navigate them? Accepting our reality allows us to find a place of calm amidst the chaos."

"Reflect on how acceptance has allowed you to find stability in your recovery. Think about how surrendering to what is, rather than resisting, has brought you a sense of relief and clarity. Acceptance is not a passive act but a powerful decision to align with reality and move forward with grace."

"Today, practice embracing acceptance as a means of fostering inner peace. Allow yourself to let go of the need for control and find comfort in the present moment. By accepting what is, you open yourself up to a more harmonious and fulfilling journey."

February 3
Finding Strength in Vulnerability

"Vulnerability is often seen as a weakness, but in reality, it's a source of immense strength. Reflect on a time when you allowed yourself to be vulnerable. How did it impact your relationships and your sense of self? Embracing vulnerability means allowing ourselves to be seen and to connect deeply with others."

"Think about the ways in which opening up to others has strengthened your support network. Vulnerability creates opportunities for genuine connections and deeper understanding. Embracing your own vulnerabilities can foster empathy and strengthen your recovery journey."

"Today, embrace your vulnerabilities with courage. Recognize them as pathways to deeper connections and personal strength. By allowing yourself to be open and honest, you invite greater compassion and support into your life."

February 4
The Journey of Forgiveness

"Forgiveness is a profound act of self-liberation. Reflect on someone or something you need to forgive. What are the barriers that have kept you from letting go? Forgiveness is not just for others; it's a gift we give to ourselves to free our hearts from the burdens of resentment."

"Consider the emotional weight of holding onto grudges. Reflect on how forgiving can lift this burden and offer you emotional freedom. Forgiveness is a healing process that allows us to release past hurts and move forward with a lighter heart."

"As you work on forgiveness today, focus on the freedom it brings to your spirit. Allow yourself to let go of past grievances and embrace the peace that comes with releasing these attachments. Forgiveness is a journey towards healing and renewal."

February 5
Embracing Your Unique Path

"Each person's recovery journey is unique. Reflect on the distinct path you are walking. How has your personal journey differed from what you expected, and how has it shaped your understanding of yourself? Embracing your unique path means recognizing and honoring your individual experiences and growth."

"Consider how acknowledging your unique journey has influenced your self-perception. Reflect on the value of your personal experiences and how they contribute to your growth. Your path is uniquely yours, and embracing it fully allows you to cultivate deeper self-awareness and appreciation."

"Today, celebrate the individuality of your journey. Recognize that your experiences and growth are valuable and worthy of recognition. Allow your unique path to guide you towards greater self-understanding and fulfillment."

February 6
The Role of Patience in Recovery

"Patience is an essential virtue on the road to recovery. Reflect on a moment when patience was especially challenging for you. What did you learn from that experience, and how did it impact your journey? Patience allows us to weather the storms and appreciate the gradual unfolding of our growth."

"Reflect on the moments when patience has been a struggle and consider what those times have taught you. Patience is about trusting the process and recognizing that progress often comes slowly. It's a practice of endurance and hope."

"Today, embrace patience as a companion on your journey. Trust that your efforts are leading you towards healing and growth. Celebrate the small victories and be gentle with yourself as you navigate the path of recovery."

February 7
The Power of Self-Reflection

"Self-reflection is a powerful tool for understanding and growth. Reflect on a recent experience that provided insight into your behavior or thought patterns. How has this reflection helped you understand yourself better? Self-reflection allows us to gain clarity and make conscious choices."

"Think about the impact of self-reflection on your journey. How has it helped you recognize patterns and make adjustments? Self-reflection is a way to engage with your inner self and gain valuable insights that support your recovery process."

"As you reflect today, approach your thoughts with curiosity and openness. Use self-reflection to explore your inner world and gain a deeper understanding of your behaviors and motivations. Allow this insight to guide your choices and enhance your journey."

February 8
Embracing the Present Moment

"The present moment is where life unfolds, and embracing it can bring profound peace. Reflect on a time when you were fully present. How did it impact your experience and your sense of well-being? Being present helps us connect with life's richness and beauty."

"Consider how focusing on the present moment has shifted your perspective. How does it help you manage stress and appreciate the beauty around you? Embracing the present moment allows us to find joy in the now and fosters a sense of contentment."

"Today, immerse yourself in the present moment. Let go of distractions and fully engage with your experiences. Celebrate the clarity and calm that come from being present and allow it to enrich your recovery journey."

February 9
Finding Meaning in Challenges

"Challenges often hold hidden opportunities for growth and learning. Reflect on a recent challenge and consider what it has taught you. How has this experience shaped your perspective and contributed to your personal development? Finding meaning in challenges helps us navigate difficulties with greater resilience."

"Reflect on how facing challenges has influenced your outlook on recovery. What insights have you gained from overcoming obstacles? Embracing challenges as opportunities for growth allows us to build strength and resilience."

"As you encounter challenges today, seek out the lessons they offer. Embrace them as opportunities for growth and transformation. Celebrate the strength and wisdom gained from facing difficulties and use these insights to support your ongoing journey."

February 10
Cultivating Inner Peace

"Inner peace is a state of being that comes from within. Reflect on practices or activities that help you cultivate a sense of inner calm. How do these practices support your emotional well-being and recovery? Cultivating inner peace involves finding tranquility amidst life's fluctuations."

"Think about the ways in which cultivating inner peace has impacted your recovery. How does it help you manage stress and maintain balance? Inner peace is a practice that requires attention and intention, fostering a serene mindset."

"Today, engage in practices that nourish your spirit and bring you tranquility. Celebrate the inner peace you cultivate and allow it to guide you through your recovery journey. Embrace the calm and clarity that come from nurturing your inner serenity."

February 11
The Importance of Self-Compassion

"Self-compassion is a crucial element of the recovery journey. Reflect on a moment when you were harsh with yourself. How did that affect your well-being? Practicing self-compassion means treating yourself with the same kindness and understanding that you would offer a friend."

"Consider how being gentle with yourself has influenced your recovery. How does self-compassion help you navigate challenges and setbacks? Cultivating a compassionate attitude towards yourself can ease the inner struggle and foster a supportive environment for healing."

"Today, embrace self-compassion as a guiding principle. Recognize your efforts and be kind to yourself, especially during difficult moments. Allow self-compassion to nurture your growth and support your journey towards recovery."

February 12
Building Resilience Through Adversity

"Resilience is built through facing and overcoming adversity. Reflect on a recent adversity you've encountered. How did you respond, and what strengths did you discover in yourself? Building resilience involves learning from challenges and emerging stronger."

"Think about how adversity has shaped your recovery. What lessons have you learned about your own resilience? Facing difficulties with courage and determination helps build a solid foundation for continued growth and recovery."

"Today, focus on the resilience you've developed through adversity. Embrace your strength and use it to navigate current challenges. Celebrate your ability to persevere and draw upon the inner resources you've cultivated."

February 13
The Art of Letting Go

"Letting go is a profound act of release and freedom. Reflect on something you're holding onto that no longer serves you. How does holding on affect your recovery and well-being? Letting go allows us to move forward and create space for new possibilities."

"Consider the ways in which releasing attachments has impacted your journey. How does it contribute to your sense of peace and progress? Letting go involves trusting the process and embracing change with an open heart."

"As you practice letting go today, focus on releasing what no longer serves you. Allow yourself to be free from burdens and open to new opportunities. Embrace the liberation that comes with letting go and moving forward."

February 14
The Healing Power of Gratitude

"Gratitude has a remarkable ability to shift our perspective and enhance our recovery. Reflect on something you are grateful for today. How does acknowledging gratitude affect your mood and outlook? Practicing gratitude can bring a sense of positivity and appreciation into our lives."

"Think about how expressing gratitude has influenced your recovery. How does it help you focus on the positive aspects of your journey? Gratitude fosters a sense of well-being and helps us recognize the support and blessings we have."

"Today, make a conscious effort to express gratitude. Notice the positive impact it has on your mindset and emotional state. Embrace the healing power of gratitude and allow it to uplift and support your recovery process."

February 15
The Journey of Self-Discovery

"Self-discovery is a continuous journey of uncovering who we are. Reflect on a recent discovery about yourself. How has this insight influenced your recovery and personal growth? Self-discovery involves exploring your values, strengths, and areas for growth."

"Consider how self-discovery has enriched your understanding of yourself. How does it impact your recovery journey and self-acceptance? Embracing the journey of self-discovery can lead to profound personal insights and empowerment."

"Today, engage in practices that support self-discovery. Explore new aspects of yourself and reflect on how they contribute to your recovery. Celebrate the insights you gain and use them to guide your personal growth."

February 16
Nurturing Healthy Boundaries

"Healthy boundaries are essential for maintaining balance and well-being. Reflect on a boundary you've set or need to set. How has establishing this boundary impacted your relationships and recovery? Nurturing healthy boundaries helps protect your emotional and physical space."

"Think about how maintaining boundaries has supported your recovery. How does it contribute to your sense of safety and self-respect? Healthy boundaries allow you to engage in relationships and activities that align with your values and needs."

"Today, focus on nurturing and respecting your boundaries. Recognize their importance in supporting your recovery and well-being. Embrace boundaries as a means of creating a balanced and fulfilling life."

February 17
The Role of Mindful Communication

"Mindful communication enhances our relationships and supports our recovery. Reflect on a recent conversation where you practiced mindful listening or speaking. How did this approach affect the interaction and your connection with others? Mindful communication involves being present and engaged in our interactions."

"Consider how mindful communication has influenced your recovery journey. How does it help you build stronger connections and resolve conflicts? Engaging in mindful communication fosters understanding and compassion in your relationships."

"Today, practice mindful communication in your interactions. Focus on listening attentively and expressing yourself clearly and thoughtfully. Embrace the benefits of mindful communication in nurturing supportive relationships and enhancing your recovery."

February 18
The Impact of Self-Acceptance

"Self-acceptance is a fundamental aspect of recovery and personal growth. Reflect on an area where you've struggled with self-acceptance. How has this struggle affected your journey? Embracing self-acceptance involves recognizing and valuing your inherent worth and imperfections."

"Think about how self-acceptance has shaped your recovery. How does it contribute to your sense of peace and confidence? Accepting yourself fully allows you to move forward with greater self-compassion and resilience."

"Today, focus on cultivating self-acceptance. Embrace your strengths and imperfections as integral parts of who you are. Celebrate your journey towards self-acceptance and allow it to support your ongoing recovery."

February 19
The Practice of Mindful Eating

"Mindful eating involves being fully present during meals and savoring each bite. Reflect on your eating habits and how mindfulness might enhance your experience. How does being present during meals contribute to your overall well-being? Mindful eating supports a healthy relationship with food and promotes awareness."

"Consider how practicing mindful eating has impacted your recovery. How does it affect your physical and emotional health? Engaging in mindful eating encourages a balanced approach to nourishment and fosters a deeper connection with your body."

"Today, practice mindful eating by focusing on the sensory experience of your meals. Pay attention to the flavors, textures, and sensations of each bite. Embrace mindful eating as a way to nurture your body and support your recovery journey."

February 20
The Power of Positive Affirmations

"Positive affirmations can shift our mindset and reinforce our goals. Reflect on a positive affirmation that resonates with you. How does repeating this affirmation influence your thoughts and actions? Positive affirmations help cultivate a mindset of optimism and self-belief."

"Think about how using positive affirmations has supported your recovery. How do they impact your self-esteem and motivation? Incorporating affirmations into your daily routine can enhance your resilience and reinforce your commitment to recovery."

"Today, use positive affirmations to uplift and inspire yourself. Repeat affirmations that resonate with your goals and aspirations. Embrace their power to shape your mindset and support your ongoing journey towards recovery."

February 21
Cultivating Joy in Daily Life

"Finding joy in daily life can significantly impact our recovery and overall well-being. Reflect on a recent moment of joy or happiness. How did it affect your mood and perspective? Cultivating joy involves recognizing and savoring the small pleasures and positive experiences in life."

"Consider how cultivating joy has influenced your recovery journey. How does it contribute to your sense of fulfillment and balance? Embracing joy helps counterbalance challenges and fosters a positive outlook."

"Today, focus on finding and celebrating moments of joy in your daily life. Engage in activities that bring you happiness and fulfillment. Allow joy to enhance your recovery and enrich your overall experience."

February 22
The Importance of Self-Care

"Self-care is an essential practice for maintaining well-being and supporting recovery. Reflect on your current self-care routine. How does it contribute to your physical and emotional health? Prioritizing self-care involves recognizing and meeting your own needs with kindness and respect."

"Think about how self-care practices have impacted your recovery journey. How do they support your resilience and sense of balance? Incorporating self-care into your routine can foster a healthier and more sustainable recovery process."

"Today, focus on self-care activities that nurture your well-being. Take time to engage in practices that support your physical and emotional health. Celebrate the importance of self-care and its role in your ongoing recovery."

February 23
The Value of Seeking Support

"Seeking support is a vital aspect of the recovery journey. Reflect on a time when reaching out for help made a difference. How did this support impact your recovery and well-being? Seeking support involves recognizing the value of connection and guidance from others."

"Consider how seeking support has influenced your recovery process. How does it contribute to your sense of belonging and empowerment? Building a network of support can provide encouragement, accountability, and valuable insights."

"Today, embrace the value of seeking support. Reach out to those who can offer guidance and encouragement. Recognize the importance of connection and allow it to strengthen your recovery journey."

February 24
The Power of Reflection and Growth

"Reflection is a powerful tool for personal growth and understanding. Reflect on your progress over the past month. What insights and lessons have you gained? Regular reflection helps us acknowledge our growth and identify areas for continued development."

"Think about how reflecting on your journey has supported your recovery. How does it help you celebrate achievements and address challenges? Embracing reflection can enhance self-awareness and foster a deeper commitment to your goals."

"Today, take time to reflect on your progress and growth. Acknowledge your achievements and consider areas for further development. Use this reflection to inspire and motivate yourself as you continue on your recovery journey."

February 25
The Practice of Mindful Breathing

"Mindful breathing is a simple yet effective practice for grounding and calming the mind. Reflect on how mindful breathing affects your stress levels and emotional state. How does focusing on your breath help you stay present and centered? Mindful breathing supports relaxation and mental clarity."

"Consider how incorporating mindful breathing into your daily routine has impacted your well-being. How does it enhance your ability to manage stress and stay focused? Practicing mindful breathing can foster a sense of calm and balance."

"Today, practice mindful breathing to cultivate a sense of tranquility. Pay attention to the rhythm of your breath and use it as a tool for grounding and relaxation. Embrace the benefits of mindful breathing for your recovery and overall well-being."

February 26
Embracing Your Journey with Compassion

"Compassion towards yourself and your journey is essential for growth and healing. Reflect on a time when you approached yourself with compassion. How did this attitude affect your recovery and sense of self? Embracing compassion involves treating yourself with kindness and understanding."

"Think about how compassion has influenced your recovery journey. How does it support your emotional well-being and resilience? Practicing self-compassion can create a nurturing environment for growth and healing."

"Today, focus on embracing your journey with compassion. Treat yourself with kindness and acknowledge the efforts you've made. Allow compassion to guide your interactions with yourself and others, supporting your ongoing recovery."

February 27
The Significance of Mindful Actions

"Mindful actions involve bringing awareness to the tasks and activities we engage in. Reflect on how being mindful during daily activities impacts your experience. How does mindfulness influence your sense of fulfillment and presence? Engaging in mindful actions enhances our connection to the present moment."

"Consider how mindful actions have affected your recovery. How does it contribute to a greater sense of satisfaction and balance? Practicing mindfulness in your actions can support a more focused and intentional approach to life."

"Today, approach your activities with mindfulness. Pay attention to the details and sensations of each action. Embrace the benefits of mindful actions for fostering a deeper connection to your daily experiences and recovery journey."

February 28
The Journey Towards Self-Discovery

"The path of self-discovery is an ongoing journey of uncovering and understanding ourselves. Reflect on a recent insight or revelation about yourself. How has this discovery influenced your perspective and recovery? Self-discovery involves exploring your values, desires, and inner strengths."

"Think about how self-discovery has enriched your journey. How does it impact your sense of purpose and direction? Embracing self-discovery can lead to greater self-awareness and personal growth."

"Today, engage in practices that support self-discovery. Explore new facets of yourself and reflect on how they contribute to your recovery. Celebrate the insights you gain and use them to guide your ongoing journey of growth and understanding."

MARCH

March 1
Embracing the Present Moment

"The present moment is the only reality we have. Reflect on how often you find yourself caught in the past or worried about the future. How does this impact your recovery and peace of mind? Learning to embrace the present allows us to live more fully and mindfully."

"Think about how living in the present moment has shaped your recovery. How does it influence your ability to cope with challenges? Embracing the now helps reduce anxiety and fosters a sense of groundedness."

"Today, practice being present in everything you do. Notice the sights, sounds, and sensations around you. Let the present moment guide you to a calmer, more centered state of being and recovery."

March 2

The Courage to Face Change

"Change can be daunting, yet it is an inevitable part of life and recovery. Reflect on a change you've been resistant to. What fears or uncertainties are holding you back? Facing change with courage opens the door to transformation and growth."

"Consider how embracing change has impacted your recovery journey. How does adapting to new circumstances help you grow stronger and more resilient? Facing change with an open heart allows you to evolve with each step forward."

"Today, focus on facing change with courage. Allow yourself to acknowledge the discomfort, but also recognize the potential for growth. Embrace change as an essential part of your recovery and personal evolution."

March 3
Releasing Perfectionism

"Perfectionism can create unnecessary pressure and hinder progress. Reflect on how the need to be perfect has impacted your recovery. How does striving for perfection affect your emotional well-being? Releasing perfectionism allows for a more compassionate, realistic approach to growth."

"Think about the times when you allowed yourself to be imperfect. How did it feel, and how did it influence your recovery? Letting go of perfectionism helps you focus on progress rather than an unattainable ideal."

"Today, practice releasing the need to be perfect. Celebrate your efforts and progress, no matter how small. Accept that imperfections are part of being human, and use them as opportunities for growth and learning."

March 4

Cultivating Patience

"Patience is a vital virtue in recovery. Reflect on a situation where impatience led to frustration or setbacks. How did this impact your progress? Cultivating patience helps us accept the pace of recovery and understand that healing takes time."

"Consider how patience has supported your recovery. How does it help you cope with challenges and delays? Embracing patience allows for a gentler, more accepting attitude toward yourself and your journey."

"Today, focus on cultivating patience. Remind yourself that recovery is a process, not a race. Allow time and persistence to guide your growth and trust that progress will come with steady effort."

March 5
Finding Peace in Silence

"Silence can offer deep insights and peace. Reflect on your relationship with silence. How often do you allow yourself to sit in stillness, free from distractions? Finding peace in silence allows you to connect with your inner self and recharge emotionally."

"Think about how moments of silence have impacted your recovery. How does embracing quiet help you reflect and gain clarity? Silence can be a powerful tool for self-discovery and emotional balance."

"Today, set aside time for silence. Turn off the noise, sit in stillness, and allow yourself to simply be. Embrace the calm and insights that arise from silence as you continue on your path to recovery."

March 6
The Role of Self-Forgiveness

"Forgiveness, especially self-forgiveness, is an essential aspect of healing. Reflect on a time when you struggled to forgive yourself. How did this affect your recovery and emotional health? Practicing self-forgiveness helps release guilt and shame, making space for growth."

"Consider how self-forgiveness has influenced your journey. How does it help you move forward with a lighter heart? Letting go of past mistakes allows you to approach recovery with greater compassion and understanding."

"Today, focus on the practice of self-forgiveness. Acknowledge your past mistakes, but choose to let them go. Embrace the freedom that comes with forgiving yourself and moving forward with renewed hope."

March 7
Strengthening Your Inner Resolve

"Inner resolve is the determination that keeps us moving forward in difficult times. Reflect on a moment in your recovery when you had to draw on your inner strength. How did this resolve help you overcome challenges? Strengthening your inner resolve provides you with the resilience needed to stay on course."

"Think about how tapping into your inner strength has affected your recovery. How does it empower you to face obstacles? Building inner resolve allows you to weather the storms of life with confidence and perseverance."

"Today, focus on strengthening your resolve. Recognize your ability to rise above difficulties and keep moving forward. Use your inner strength as a compass to guide you through challenges on your recovery journey."

March 8
The Power of Vulnerability

"Vulnerability is often seen as a weakness, but in reality, it is a source of great strength. Reflect on a time when you allowed yourself to be vulnerable. How did this openness impact your recovery and relationships? Embracing vulnerability fosters authenticity and deeper connections with others."

"Consider how being vulnerable has shaped your recovery journey. How does it help you build trust and find support? Vulnerability allows for emotional healing and invites others to share in your experience with compassion."

"Today, embrace the power of vulnerability. Allow yourself to open up, share your truth, and connect with others on a deeper level. Trust that vulnerability is a strength, not a weakness, and let it support your recovery."

March 9

Recognizing Progress Over Perfection

"It's easy to get caught up in the pursuit of perfection, but progress is what truly matters. Reflect on the progress you've made in your recovery, even if it feels small. How does acknowledging progress affect your motivation and self-esteem? Recognizing progress helps you stay focused on growth instead of unrealistic ideals."

"Think about how celebrating progress has influenced your recovery. How does it shift your mindset from frustration to encouragement? Focusing on small victories builds confidence and sustains your momentum."

"Today, celebrate the progress you've made, no matter how minor it may seem. Recognize that each step forward is a victory on your journey. Let progress be your guide, and release the pressure of perfection."

March 10
Balancing Effort and Rest

"In recovery, it's important to find balance between effort and rest. Reflect on how much energy you're dedicating to your recovery and whether you're allowing yourself time to rest. How does finding balance impact your overall well-being? Rest is essential for replenishment, while effort propels you forward."

"Consider how balancing effort and rest has supported your recovery. How does it help prevent burnout and maintain your focus? Striking a balance allows you to sustain your energy and motivation over the long term."

"Today, focus on finding a balance between effort and rest. Recognize when it's time to push forward and when it's time to pause. Let this balance support your recovery and contribute to your overall sense of well-being."

March 11
Letting Go of Control

"The need to control everything can often lead to frustration and disappointment. Reflect on a situation in which you tried to control the outcome. How did this affect your mental state and your recovery? Letting go of control allows us to trust the process and embrace uncertainty."

"Consider how releasing control has impacted your recovery. How does surrendering the need to dictate every outcome bring peace and relief? Trusting in the natural flow of life enables a sense of freedom and ease in your journey."

"Today, practice letting go of control. Accept that you cannot manage every detail or force specific outcomes. Allow life to unfold naturally, and trust that your recovery will follow the path that's right for you."

March 12

The Power of Consistency

"Consistency is key to long-term growth and recovery. Reflect on your daily habits and the areas where you've maintained consistency. How has this steady effort influenced your progress? Building consistent habits reinforces stability and growth in your recovery."

"Think about how being consistent has shaped your journey. How does it affect your confidence and sense of accomplishment? Consistency creates a foundation that supports continued success in recovery."

"Today, focus on reinforcing consistency in your actions and habits. Acknowledge the areas where you've been steady, and build upon them. Let consistency be the thread that ties together your recovery and personal development."

March 13
The Healing Power of Gratitude

"Gratitude has the power to shift our perspective and promote healing. Reflect on something in your life that you feel grateful for today. How does practicing gratitude influence your mood and recovery? Gratitude allows us to see the good, even in challenging times, and fosters a sense of contentment."

"Consider how gratitude has affected your recovery journey. How does it help you focus on the positive and maintain a hopeful outlook? Practicing gratitude invites joy and appreciation into your life, supporting emotional healing."

"Today, cultivate an attitude of gratitude. Take a moment to reflect on what you're thankful for, no matter how small. Allow gratitude to be a source of comfort and healing as you continue on your path to recovery."

March 14

Embracing Impermanence

"Everything in life is constantly changing, and embracing impermanence can bring peace. Reflect on how you react to change or loss. How does accepting impermanence affect your recovery? Understanding that everything is temporary helps us let go of attachments and live with more ease."

"Think about how recognizing impermanence has shaped your perspective. How does it help you navigate challenges and transitions in recovery? Accepting the ebb and flow of life can lead to a deeper sense of peace and acceptance."

"Today, embrace the concept of impermanence. Acknowledge that both joy and hardship are temporary. Let this understanding guide you toward greater balance and serenity in your recovery journey."

March 15
Trusting the Process

"Recovery is a journey that unfolds over time. Reflect on how trusting the process has impacted your experience. How does faith in your progress help you stay grounded and hopeful? Trusting the process allows us to relinquish control and focus on steady progress."

"Consider how trusting the process has influenced your recovery. How does it shift your perspective from impatience to patience? Believing in the process fosters resilience and prevents discouragement."

"Today, practice trusting the process. Acknowledge that recovery takes time and that each step, no matter how small, is meaningful. Let your trust in the journey guide you through challenges with patience and faith."

March 16
The Gift of Humility

"Humility allows us to see ourselves clearly, without the ego's distortions. Reflect on a time when you embraced humility in your recovery. How did this openness impact your relationships and self-awareness? Humility helps us stay grounded, open to learning, and connected to others."

"Think about how practicing humility has shaped your recovery. How does it help you stay honest and accountable? Embracing humility allows for growth and fosters a deeper connection with your true self."

"Today, focus on cultivating humility. Recognize that you are both strong and fallible, and that growth comes from learning. Use humility as a tool for deepening your recovery and relationships."

March 17
Building Emotional Resilience

"Emotional resilience is the ability to bounce back from challenges. Reflect on a time when you faced emotional adversity. How did your resilience help you navigate this experience? Building emotional resilience strengthens your ability to cope with the ups and downs of recovery."
"Consider how resilience has impacted your recovery journey. How does it help you stay focused on healing, even during difficult moments? Emotional resilience empowers you to face setbacks with courage and determination."
"Today, focus on building emotional resilience. Embrace the idea that challenges are a natural part of life, and trust in your ability to rise above them. Let resilience be the foundation for your ongoing recovery."

March 18

The Importance of Accountability

"Accountability keeps us grounded and responsible for our actions. Reflect on how accountability has played a role in your recovery. How does being accountable to yourself and others strengthen your commitment to growth? Practicing accountability encourages honesty and fosters trust."

"Think about how accountability has influenced your recovery. How does it help you stay on track and maintain integrity? Holding yourself accountable allows for greater transparency and supports long-term success."

"Today, focus on maintaining accountability. Be honest with yourself about your progress and challenges. Use accountability as a tool to support your recovery and strengthen your commitment to personal growth."

March 19

The Freedom of Acceptance

"Acceptance brings a sense of freedom and peace. Reflect on an area of your life that you've struggled to accept. How has this resistance affected your recovery? Embracing acceptance allows us to let go of what we cannot control and focus on what we can change."

"Consider how practicing acceptance has influenced your recovery journey. How does it help you find peace and clarity? Accepting reality as it is opens the door to inner calm and frees us from unnecessary suffering."

"Today, practice the freedom of acceptance. Acknowledge the things you cannot change and focus on what is within your power. Let acceptance guide you toward greater peace and ease in your recovery process."

March 20
The Role of Self-Reflection

"Self-reflection is a powerful tool for personal growth. Reflect on how often you take time to self-reflect. How does this practice influence your recovery? Engaging in self-reflection helps you gain insights into your thoughts, behaviors, and emotions, leading to greater self-awareness."

"Think about how self-reflection has shaped your recovery journey. How does it help you stay mindful and make intentional decisions? Practicing self-reflection allows for deeper understanding and more thoughtful action."

"Today, take time for self-reflection. Use this moment to check in with yourself, assess your progress, and consider areas for growth. Let self-reflection be a guiding force in your recovery and personal evolution."

March 21
Living with Intention

"Setting intentions brings purpose to our actions. Reflect on the last time you set a clear intention for your recovery. How did this focus shape your day or week? Living with intention helps us make mindful choices that align with our values and goals."

"Consider how setting intentions has impacted your recovery. How does being purposeful in your actions make a difference in your overall well-being? With clear intentions, you create a path that leads you toward growth and healing."

"Today, set a positive intention for your recovery. Let this intention guide your actions and decisions throughout the day. Focus on aligning your behavior with the values that are important to you."

March 22
Finding Strength in Vulnerability

"Vulnerability often feels like a weakness, but it can be a source of great strength. Reflect on a time when you allowed yourself to be vulnerable. How did this openness lead to deeper connections or personal growth? Being vulnerable in recovery allows us to heal and connect authentically."

"Think about how embracing vulnerability has helped your recovery process. How does it foster trust and honesty with yourself and others? Vulnerability invites deeper understanding and a sense of belonging."

"Today, explore the strength in vulnerability. Allow yourself to be open and honest about your feelings, even if it feels uncomfortable. Trust that vulnerability can lead to healing and stronger relationships in your recovery."

March 23
The Value of Patience

"Recovery is a journey, not a destination, and patience is essential. Reflect on a situation where you felt impatient with your progress. How did this impatience affect your mental state? Patience reminds us that growth happens gradually, and rushing can hinder our recovery."

"Consider how patience has played a role in your recovery. How does slowing down and allowing things to unfold at their own pace support your healing? Patience creates space for sustainable change and long-term success."

"Today, practice patience in your recovery. Acknowledge that every step forward, no matter how small, is progress. Allow yourself the grace to move through the process without rushing or forcing outcomes."

March 24
The Practice of Forgiveness

"Forgiveness is a powerful tool for releasing pain and resentment. Reflect on someone, including yourself, that you've struggled to forgive. How has holding onto this resentment impacted your recovery? Forgiving doesn't mean condoning harm, but it allows us to let go of the emotional weight."

"Think about how forgiveness has influenced your journey. How does forgiving others, and yourself, bring peace and clarity to your recovery? Forgiveness clears the path to emotional freedom and healing."

"Today, practice forgiveness. Start by acknowledging the pain, and then work toward releasing it. Let forgiveness be an act of self-compassion and a step toward emotional liberation."

March 25
Building Inner Peace

"Inner peace isn't something we find externally; it's something we cultivate within ourselves. Reflect on a moment when you felt true peace. What contributed to that feeling, and how can you recreate it in your recovery? Inner peace provides a stable foundation for growth and resilience."

"Consider how inner peace has influenced your recovery. How does cultivating calmness and serenity in your mind help you navigate challenges? Inner peace strengthens your ability to remain grounded, even in turbulent times."

"Today, focus on building inner peace. Engage in practices that calm your mind, such as meditation or mindful breathing. Let peace be your guide as you continue along your path to recovery."

March 26
Releasing Self-Judgment

"Self-judgment can be one of the biggest obstacles in recovery. Reflect on a moment when you were particularly hard on yourself. How did this self-criticism affect your progress? Releasing judgment allows us to approach recovery with kindness and acceptance."

"Think about how reducing self-judgment has helped your recovery. How does being compassionate toward yourself encourage personal growth? Letting go of harsh self-criticism opens the door to greater self-acceptance and healing."

"Today, work on releasing self-judgment. Speak to yourself with the same kindness and understanding you would offer a loved one. Allow self-compassion to fuel your recovery and your relationship with yourself."

March 27
The Role of Surrender

"Surrendering in recovery doesn't mean giving up; it means letting go of control over things you cannot change. Reflect on a time when you struggled to surrender to a situation. How did holding on affect you? Surrendering allows us to find peace in acceptance."

"Consider how surrender has influenced your journey. How does it help you let go of resistance and focus on what's truly important? Surrender opens space for growth by freeing you from the burden of control."

"Today, practice surrender. Acknowledge the things that are beyond your control, and release your need to manage them. Let surrender bring you closer to peace and clarity in your recovery."

March 28

Embracing Uncertainty

"Recovery can be an uncertain path, and learning to embrace that uncertainty is crucial. Reflect on how you handle the unknown in your life. How does uncertainty affect your recovery process? Embracing uncertainty teaches us to navigate change and unpredictability with grace."

"Think about how accepting uncertainty has shaped your recovery. How does letting go of the need for certainty free you from fear and anxiety? Learning to live with the unknown strengthens resilience and flexibility."

"Today, embrace uncertainty as a natural part of life. Instead of fearing the unknown, approach it with curiosity and openness. Let this acceptance guide you toward greater peace and adaptability in your recovery journey."

March 29
The Gift of Self-Compassion

"Self-compassion is essential in recovery. Reflect on how you've shown yourself kindness and compassion during difficult times. How has this self-care supported your healing process? Self-compassion helps us approach our struggles with gentleness rather than harsh criticism."

"Consider how self-compassion has impacted your recovery. How does being kind to yourself foster emotional healing and resilience? Practicing self-compassion nurtures a sense of inner strength and self-worth."

"Today, focus on extending compassion toward yourself. Whether you're facing challenges or celebrating progress, treat yourself with the same care you would offer to others. Let self-compassion be a powerful tool in your recovery."

March 30
The Importance of Staying Present

"In recovery, staying present helps us avoid being overwhelmed by the past or future. Reflect on a moment when you were truly present. How did this mindfulness affect your recovery? Staying in the present moment allows us to focus on what we can control right now."

"Think about how practicing presence has shaped your journey. How does staying grounded in the moment prevent distraction and stress? Mindfulness strengthens your ability to manage each day with clarity and focus."

"Today, commit to staying present. Bring your awareness to the here and now, and release concerns about what has been or what might be. Let the present moment guide your recovery and provide peace of mind."

March 31
The Journey of Self-Discovery

"Recovery is a process of rediscovering who we truly are. Reflect on what you've learned about yourself during your recovery. How has this self-awareness helped you grow? The journey of self-discovery is ongoing, and each day offers new insights."

"Consider how self-discovery has influenced your recovery. How does learning more about your strengths, weaknesses, and desires help you navigate your healing process? Self-awareness deepens your connection to your true self and supports lasting change."

"Today, embrace the journey of self-discovery. Take time to reflect on what you've learned about yourself, and celebrate your growth. Let self-awareness be a guiding light as you continue on the path of recovery and transformation."

APRIL

April 1
Awakening to Self-Acceptance

"Self-acceptance is the foundation of growth. Reflect on how you perceive yourself today. What parts of yourself do you struggle to accept? Embracing who you are, flaws and all, is the first step toward genuine healing and change."

"Consider how self-acceptance has played a role in your recovery. How does accepting both your strengths and weaknesses free you from self-criticism? Through acceptance, we find the peace and courage to move forward."

"Today, practice self-acceptance by acknowledging your worth without judgment. Rather than focusing on who you think you should be, honor who you are in this moment. Let acceptance guide you toward greater compassion for yourself."

April 2
Letting Go of Control

"In recovery, the desire to control everything can create unnecessary tension. Reflect on a situation where you found it hard to relinquish control. How did holding on tightly affect your emotional state? Letting go of control allows you to embrace peace in uncertainty."

"Think about how releasing control has positively impacted your recovery. How does allowing things to unfold naturally create space for growth and healing? Letting go provides the freedom to focus on what truly matters."

"Today, practice releasing control over situations beyond your reach. Trust the process and focus on your own actions rather than the outcomes. Let go, and allow yourself to flow with life instead of resisting it."

April 3
Compassion for Others

"Compassion isn't just about empathy; it's about seeing the humanity in others. Reflect on a time when you showed compassion toward someone in need. How did this act affect your relationship with them and yourself? Compassion strengthens bonds and fosters understanding."

"Consider how compassion toward others has influenced your recovery. How does extending kindness and empathy help you grow emotionally? Compassion opens the heart and deepens connections, making recovery a shared experience."

"Today, extend compassion toward someone in your life. Whether through a kind word or a helpful gesture, focus on the humanity of others. Let compassion become a part of your daily practice, both in and out of recovery."

April 4
Embracing Change

"Change can feel overwhelming, but it's a necessary part of recovery. Reflect on a recent change in your life, whether big or small. How did you react to it, and what did you learn from the experience? Embracing change helps us grow and adapt to new possibilities."

"Think about how embracing change has shaped your recovery. How does being open to transformation lead to new opportunities for healing? Change is not something to fear, but something to welcome with grace and curiosity."

"Today, embrace change in your life, no matter how uncomfortable it may feel. Instead of resisting, lean into the uncertainty with an open mind. Let change lead you toward new growth and deeper understanding."

April 5
The Power of Gratitude

"Gratitude is a practice that shifts our perspective from lack to abundance. Reflect on something in your life that you feel grateful for. How does focusing on gratitude change your mood and outlook? Gratitude helps us see the beauty and value in what we already have."

"Consider how gratitude has influenced your recovery. How does focusing on what you appreciate rather than what you lack foster a sense of peace? Gratitude grounds us in the present and brings joy to the recovery process."

"Today, practice gratitude by naming three things you're thankful for. Whether big or small, let these blessings be a source of comfort and joy. Let gratitude guide you through your day, helping you stay connected to what truly matters."

April 6
Rebuilding Trust in Yourself

"Trust in oneself is often eroded by addiction, but it can be rebuilt. Reflect on a moment when you doubted yourself. How did this lack of trust affect your recovery? Rebuilding self-trust is essential for personal growth and progress."

"Think about how rebuilding trust in yourself has contributed to your recovery. How does learning to rely on your own strength and judgment help you feel more empowered? Trust in yourself strengthens your resilience and confidence."

"Today, focus on rebuilding self-trust. Start by acknowledging the small victories in your recovery journey. With each step forward, remind yourself that you are capable and worthy of trust."

April 7
The Practice of Mindful Listening

"Mindful listening means being fully present in conversations without judgment or distraction. Reflect on a time when you truly listened to someone. How did this deepen your connection and understanding? Mindful listening helps build empathy and strengthens relationships."

"Consider how mindful listening has supported your recovery. How does giving others your full attention create a sense of shared understanding? Listening with mindfulness opens space for deeper communication and connection."

"Today, practice mindful listening with someone in your life. Set aside your distractions and listen with curiosity and openness. Let this practice enhance your relationships and foster compassion in your recovery journey."

April 8
Facing Fear with Courage

"Fear is a natural part of life, but courage allows us to face it head-on. Reflect on a fear that has been holding you back in your recovery. How has this fear affected your decisions and actions? Facing fear with courage creates space for growth and healing."

"Think about how facing your fears has shaped your recovery process. How does stepping out of your comfort zone lead to new discoveries about yourself? Courage is not the absence of fear, but the willingness to move forward despite it."

"Today, take a small step toward facing a fear that's been holding you back. Whether it's a conversation, a decision, or a change, meet it with courage. Let this act of bravery remind you of your strength in recovery."

April 9
Honoring Your Boundaries

"Boundaries are essential for protecting our well-being in recovery. Reflect on a boundary you've set for yourself or others. How has maintaining this boundary supported your mental and emotional health? Honoring your boundaries helps you stay grounded and empowered."

"Consider how setting boundaries has influenced your recovery. How does defining your limits create a sense of safety and respect? Healthy boundaries protect your energy and allow for more authentic relationships."

"Today, focus on honoring your boundaries. Whether it's saying no or setting limits, stand firm in what you need to protect your peace. Let boundaries become a tool for maintaining balance and self-respect."

April 10
The Journey of Self-Awareness

"Self-awareness is a powerful tool for growth and healing. Reflect on what you've learned about yourself through your recovery journey. How has this self-awareness helped you navigate your challenges? The more we understand ourselves, the better equipped we are to make positive changes."

"Think about how self-awareness has shaped your recovery. How does recognizing your patterns, triggers, and strengths support your healing process? Self-awareness brings clarity and empowers you to make choices that align with your values."

"Today, take time to reflect on your journey of self-awareness. Notice any patterns or insights that have emerged, and celebrate the growth you've experienced. Let self-awareness continue to guide you as you move forward in your recovery."

April 11
Finding Peace in Forgiveness

"Forgiveness is a gift you give to yourself, not just to others. Reflect on someone, including yourself, whom you've had difficulty forgiving. How has holding onto resentment affected your recovery? Forgiveness opens the heart and allows peace to enter."

"Think about how practicing forgiveness has supported your healing process. How does letting go of grudges free you from emotional burdens? Forgiveness is not about excusing harm but releasing its hold on you."

"Today, take a step toward forgiveness. Whether it's a person, a situation, or yourself, begin by offering compassion and understanding. Let forgiveness create space for healing and renewal in your recovery."

April 12
The Strength of Vulnerability

"Vulnerability is often mistaken for weakness, but it takes great courage to be open. Reflect on a time when you allowed yourself to be vulnerable. How did this choice impact your relationships and recovery? Embracing vulnerability deepens connection and strengthens trust."

"Consider how vulnerability has helped you grow in your recovery. How does sharing your true self with others lead to greater support and understanding? Vulnerability is not about exposing weakness but about showing your strength in honesty."

"Today, practice vulnerability by sharing a part of yourself with someone you trust. Let this act of openness bring you closer to others and remind you of the power of authentic connection."

April 13
The Art of Letting Go

"Letting go isn't just about releasing control; it's about making space for something new. Reflect on a situation or feeling you've been holding onto. How has clinging to it created stress or tension in your recovery? Letting go frees you from unnecessary burdens."

"Think about how the practice of letting go has influenced your recovery journey. How does releasing what no longer serves you open doors to healing and growth? Letting go is an act of faith in the process of transformation."

"Today, choose something you're ready to let go of, whether it's a habit, belief, or relationship. Trust that by releasing it, you are creating space for something better. Let go, and allow the freedom to flow into your life."

April 14
Nurturing Patience in Recovery

"Recovery is not a race, and patience is a key to long-term success. Reflect on an area of your life where impatience has created frustration. How has the desire for immediate results affected your peace of mind? Patience allows growth to unfold naturally, in its own time."

"Consider how practicing patience has benefited your recovery. How does slowing down and trusting the process help you stay centered and calm? Patience is not about waiting; it's about finding peace in the present moment."

"Today, nurture patience in your recovery by letting go of urgency. Trust that everything will happen in its own time. With patience, you'll find the strength to persevere through challenges and celebrate small victories."

April 15
The Balance Between Effort and Surrender

"Recovery requires both effort and surrender, a delicate balance of action and acceptance. Reflect on how you've navigated this balance in your journey. How has trying to force things created stress, while surrendering to the process brought peace? Finding balance allows for both growth and serenity."

"Think about how balancing effort and surrender has shaped your recovery. How does knowing when to act and when to let go support your well-being? The dance between effort and surrender is key to finding harmony in life and recovery."

"Today, focus on finding balance between effort and surrender. Where can you take action, and where can you let go? Let this balance guide you toward a more peaceful and effective recovery process."

April 16
Finding Joy in the Present Moment

"Joy can be found in the simplest of moments, but we often overlook it. Reflect on a moment recently when you felt true joy. How did being present allow you to experience it fully? Joy lives in the here and now, not in the past or future."

"Consider how finding joy in the present has supported your recovery. How does being mindful of each moment open you to more happiness and contentment? Joy is always available to us when we are fully present."

"Today, practice finding joy in the present moment. Whether it's through a mindful breath, a smile, or an act of kindness, let joy be your guide. Embrace the small, joyful moments that are already present in your life and recovery."

April 17
Embracing Impermanence

"Nothing in life is permanent, and embracing this truth can free us from suffering. Reflect on a time when you struggled with change or loss. How did accepting impermanence help you move forward in your recovery? Understanding impermanence helps us let go of attachment and fear."

"Think about how embracing impermanence has impacted your recovery. How does knowing that both joy and pain are temporary bring comfort and resilience? Impermanence is a reminder to cherish the present without clinging to it."

"Today, embrace impermanence by letting go of the need to hold onto things or outcomes. Trust that everything is in a state of flow, and that change is a natural part of life. Let impermanence remind you to live fully and without attachment."

April 18
The Power of Meditation

"Meditation is a practice of turning inward and cultivating awareness. Reflect on how meditation has supported your recovery so far. How has sitting in stillness helped you gain clarity or calm? Meditation is a tool for healing, grounding, and self-discovery."

"Consider how the power of meditation has unfolded in your life. How does making time for stillness help you reconnect with yourself and your values? Meditation helps quiet the noise of the mind and brings us back to the essence of who we are."

"Today, deepen your meditation practice by dedicating time to sit in stillness. Whether for five minutes or an hour, allow yourself to be fully present with your breath and thoughts. Let meditation be a source of strength and serenity in your recovery."

April 19
Practicing Humility

"Humility is about recognizing our true place in the world, neither overestimating nor underestimating ourselves. Reflect on a time when humility helped you in your recovery. How did letting go of pride or self-judgment open you to new insights? Humility grounds us in reality and fosters growth."

"Think about how practicing humility has supported your recovery journey. How does acknowledging your strengths and limitations with honesty help you stay balanced? Humility brings us closer to ourselves and others, fostering connection and understanding."

"Today, practice humility by being honest with yourself about your strengths and areas for growth. Approach your recovery with a spirit of openness and willingness to learn. Let humility be your guide as you continue on your path."

April 20
Living with Integrity

"Integrity means aligning your actions with your values, even when no one is watching. Reflect on how living with integrity has influenced your recovery. How has staying true to your principles helped you build trust in yourself and others? Integrity creates a strong foundation for lasting change."

"Consider how practicing integrity has shaped your life and recovery. How does making decisions based on your values foster self-respect and accountability? Living with integrity strengthens your resolve and brings clarity to your choices."

"Today, focus on living with integrity in every aspect of your life. Let your actions reflect your deepest values, and honor the commitments you've made to yourself. With integrity, you build a life rooted in truth and purpose."

April 21
The Courage to Start Again

"Recovery is not linear, and setbacks can feel discouraging. Reflect on a time when you had to start over in some aspect of your recovery. How did facing this challenge help you grow stronger? Starting again takes courage and resilience."

"Consider how embracing new beginnings has shaped your recovery journey. How does allowing yourself to try again, without judgment, open doors for healing? Each time you start over, you bring new wisdom and strength to your path."

"Today, if you feel the need to start again, do so with compassion. Let go of any shame or guilt, and recognize the courage it takes to begin anew. Every step forward, no matter how small, is a step toward recovery."

April 22
Trusting the Process

"Recovery can be uncertain, and it's easy to doubt the journey. Reflect on a time when you struggled with trusting the process. How did this hesitation impact your progress? Trusting the process means accepting that growth happens in its own time."

"Think about how trusting the process has supported your recovery. How does letting go of the need for control and trusting in the unfolding help you stay grounded? Trust creates space for patience and perseverance."

"Today, practice trusting the process of your recovery. Even if the path ahead seems unclear, have faith that you are moving in the right direction. Trust that each step is leading you toward healing and transformation."

April 23
The Gift of Presence

"Being fully present in each moment allows us to connect more deeply with ourselves and others. Reflect on how practicing presence has influenced your recovery. How does being mindful of your thoughts, feelings, and actions support your healing? Presence is a gift we give to ourselves and those around us."

"Consider how cultivating presence has helped you navigate challenges in recovery. How does staying connected to the present moment offer clarity and peace? In each moment, we find the opportunity for growth and understanding."

"Today, give yourself the gift of presence. Slow down and be fully engaged in whatever you are doing, whether it's a conversation, a task, or simply breathing. Let presence guide you toward a deeper sense of peace and connection."

April 24
Facing Fear with Compassion

"Fear can be a powerful force in our lives, but we can meet it with compassion. Reflect on a fear you've faced during your recovery. How did confronting it with kindness help you move through it? Compassion helps us soften fear's grip and allows us to approach it with understanding."

"Think about how facing fear with compassion has supported your recovery. How does offering yourself kindness in moments of fear change the way you experience it? Compassion turns fear from an enemy into a teacher."

"Today, if fear arises, meet it with compassion. Acknowledge its presence without judgment, and offer yourself the understanding you need to move through it. Let compassion guide you through the challenges of fear."

April 25
The Practice of Gratitude

"Gratitude shifts our focus from what we lack to what we have. Reflect on how practicing gratitude has shaped your recovery. How has focusing on the positive aspects of your life and progress supported your healing? Gratitude creates space for joy and contentment."

"Consider how the practice of gratitude has helped you stay grounded in recovery. How does acknowledging what you're thankful for, no matter how small, bring a sense of fulfillment? Gratitude reminds us of the abundance in our lives, even in difficult times."

"Today, take a moment to practice gratitude. Write down or reflect on three things you're grateful for, and allow that feeling to fill you. Let gratitude become a daily practice that nurtures your recovery and well-being."

April 26
The Wisdom of Silence

"Silence can be a powerful teacher, offering us space to listen to our inner wisdom. Reflect on how silence has played a role in your recovery. How has spending time in quiet helped you gain clarity or find peace? In the stillness, we hear the truth more clearly."

"Consider how the practice of silence has supported your healing journey. How does creating space for quiet reflection help you reconnect with your intentions and values? Silence is a doorway to insight and inner calm."

"Today, embrace the wisdom of silence. Whether through meditation or simply sitting quietly, give yourself time to be still. Let silence guide you to deeper understanding and peace in your recovery."

April 27
Honoring Your Strength

"Recovery takes immense strength, even when we don't recognize it in ourselves. Reflect on a time when you demonstrated strength in your recovery. How did acknowledging this strength help you move forward? Honoring our inner strength empowers us to keep going, even in tough times."

"Think about how recognizing your strength has influenced your recovery. How does affirming your resilience help you face new challenges with confidence? Strength is not just in the big moments but in the small, daily efforts to stay on the path."

"Today, take time to honor your strength. Acknowledge the courage and resilience it has taken to come this far. Let this recognition fuel your confidence and remind you that you have the power to continue growing and healing."

April 28
The Freedom of Acceptance

"Acceptance is not about giving up; it's about embracing reality as it is. Reflect on a situation where acceptance helped you find peace in recovery. How did letting go of resistance allow you to move forward? Acceptance frees us from the burden of trying to control what we cannot change."

"Consider how practicing acceptance has supported your healing journey. How does accepting yourself, your circumstances, and others bring more peace into your life? Acceptance creates a foundation for growth and opens the door to new possibilities."

"Today, practice acceptance in an area of your life where you've been struggling. Allow yourself to release the need for control, and trust that things are unfolding as they should. Let acceptance bring you peace and freedom in your recovery."

April 29
The Gift of Compassionate Listening

"Listening with compassion is an act of love, both for ourselves and others. Reflect on a time when someone truly listened to you during your recovery. How did this experience of being heard help you heal? Compassionate listening creates space for understanding and connection."

"Think about how practicing compassionate listening has supported your recovery relationships. How does offering others your full attention and empathy deepen your connection with them? Listening without judgment is a gift that nurtures trust and care."

"Today, practice compassionate listening with someone in your life. Whether in a conversation with a loved one or a meeting with a fellow traveler on the recovery path, offer your full attention and empathy. Let compassionate listening be a healing presence in your interactions."

April 30
The Journey Continues

"Recovery is a lifelong journey, with each day offering new lessons and opportunities. Reflect on how far you've come since the start of your recovery. How have you grown, changed, and healed? The journey continues, but each step brings new strength and wisdom."

"Consider how recognizing the ongoing nature of recovery has shaped your outlook. How does seeing recovery as a process, rather than a destination, bring you peace? The journey is one of continuous growth, and each day is a chance to start anew."

"Today, honor the journey you are on. Acknowledge the progress you've made and the lessons you've learned. Trust that the road ahead holds even more possibilities for healing and transformation. The journey continues, and so do you."

MAY

May 1

Revisiting the Past with Compassion

"The past is often where we store our regrets, mistakes, and pain. But what if we could look back with compassion instead of judgment? Today, I reflect on moments I once labeled as failures and see them for what they are: lessons, guides, and opportunities to grow."

"I am not that person anymore, yet those experiences shaped the person I've become. What if each challenge was a doorway to understanding myself more deeply? My past doesn't define me, but it informs the wisdom I carry now."

"Today, I choose to greet my past with kindness. Not to dwell, but to learn. What do I need to release? And what can I embrace as a stepping stone toward healing?"

May 2
The Present as a Gift

"It's easy to get caught up in what was or what might be. But right now, I have this moment, and it's enough. I look at today as a chance to breathe, to simply exist without needing to fix anything. Can I allow this moment to be exactly as it is?"

"In this stillness, I remember that everything is transient. The struggles, the joys, the questions—they all come and go. What remains is my ability to face this day with clarity and intention. I don't need to solve the future today; I only need to live in this breath."

"I remind myself that peace is found in the present. I don't need to rush into tomorrow. I can choose to be here, now, fully present."

May 3
Navigating Uncertainty with Grace

"The unknown is uncomfortable. I've always wanted certainty, something solid to hold onto in the chaos. But in recovery, I've learned that life doesn't always offer certainty. How do I navigate that space between what I know and what I fear?"

"Instead of resisting uncertainty, I've started to view it as an invitation—a space to grow, to trust myself, and to lean into the process. My fear of the unknown has taught me that not knowing is part of the journey."

"Today, I walk with grace through uncertainty. I remind myself that I don't need all the answers to move forward. I only need to trust the path ahead, even if it's unclear."

May 4
The Power of Choice

"Every day offers choices. Some feel small, almost insignificant, but each one contributes to the larger picture of who I am becoming. In recovery, I've learned that every choice I make either brings me closer to healing or pulls me further away."

"I reflect on the power of these choices. I can choose to listen to my body, to pause before reacting, to show up for myself in ways I never did before. It's empowering to realize that I have agency in how my story unfolds."

"Today, I commit to making mindful choices. I will choose what nurtures my spirit and supports my recovery, knowing that every choice matters."

May 5
Embracing Change

"Change is uncomfortable, but it's also inevitable. I think about the changes I've resisted in the past and how they ultimately shaped my growth. Each transition, though challenging, brought me to a new level of understanding."

"The fear of change used to paralyze me, but now, I see it as part of the healing process. Without change, there's no movement, no transformation. What if change is exactly what I need?"

"Today, I open myself to the possibility that change can be my greatest ally. I will allow life to flow, even if it means letting go of the familiar."

May 6
The Weight of Expectations

"I've carried expectations for most of my life—of myself, of others, of how things should be. But these expectations often lead to disappointment when reality doesn't match the story in my head. How much of my suffering comes from holding on to what I think should happen?"

"In recovery, I've learned to let go of rigid expectations and replace them with acceptance. Life doesn't always follow my script, and that's okay. What if I could approach today without expectation, but with openness instead?"

"Today, I release the weight of unrealistic expectations. I will allow life to unfold as it will, trusting that it's exactly as it's meant to be."

May 7
Listening to My Inner Voice

"There's a voice inside of me, one that often gets drowned out by noise—my worries, distractions, and fears. But in moments of stillness, I hear it. It's a quiet, persistent voice that knows what I need, even when I don't."

"I've spent years ignoring that inner guidance, but now, I'm learning to trust it. It speaks with wisdom, reminding me of my worth and my strength. Listening to this voice is an act of self-respect and self-care."

"Today, I will take time to listen to my inner voice. I will honor its message, knowing that it's leading me toward peace and clarity."

May 8
Releasing the Need for Perfection

"Perfectionism has always been a heavy burden, one that makes me feel like I'm never enough. But in recovery, I've come to understand that perfection is an illusion—one that keeps me trapped in a cycle of self-criticism."

"What if I allowed myself to be imperfect? To make mistakes, to be messy, to not have it all figured out? In letting go of perfection, I open the door to growth and learning. My worth is not tied to how perfectly I navigate this journey."

"Today, I release the need to be perfect. I will embrace my humanity, my flaws, and my imperfections, knowing that they are part of what makes me whole."

May 9
Building Resilience

"Resilience is not something I was born with; it's something I've cultivated through hardship. Every setback, every challenge has taught me how to stand back up. I've learned that resilience is about more than just surviving—it's about thriving in the face of adversity."

"I reflect on the moments that tested my strength, and I see now that each one was an opportunity to grow. I didn't always recognize it at the time, but looking back, I see how those challenges built the resilience I have today."

"Today, I honor my resilience. I will face whatever comes my way with the knowledge that I am capable of enduring and growing through it."

May 10
The Healing Power of Forgiveness

"Forgiveness is not easy, especially when the pain runs deep. But I've learned that holding onto resentment only harms me. It keeps me tethered to the past, unable to move forward. Forgiveness is not about excusing the harm—it's about freeing myself from its hold."

"I reflect on those I need to forgive, including myself. Can I extend the same compassion to others that I would want for myself? In forgiving, I let go of the hurt and make room for healing."

"Today, I will practice forgiveness, starting with myself. I will release the past and open my heart to the possibility of peace."

May 11
Finding Strength in Vulnerability

Vulnerability is often seen as a weakness, but it is one of the greatest strengths. It allows for connection, healing, and growth. Being open to vulnerability creates space for genuine relationships and deeper understanding. Instead of hiding wounds, acknowledging them fosters resilience. Life offers moments that call for walls to come down and for real emotions to surface. In those moments, transformation occurs, not through hiding but through embracing what's raw and real. Vulnerability, though difficult, is the foundation for lasting recovery.

Trust that vulnerability is not the enemy. It's the key to unlocking inner strength and authentic living. True healing comes from embracing the full range of emotions and experiences.

May 12
Embracing Life's Transience

Nothing in life stays the same; everything is in constant motion. Change is the essence of existence, and resisting it only causes suffering. Accepting the impermanence of all things allows for peace in the present moment. Clinging to what was or what might be creates unnecessary burdens.

Each day presents a new opportunity to accept the flow of life. In this acceptance, freedom is found. Worry about the future or attachment to the past fades when embracing life's transience. It's through this understanding that the heart can fully open.

Letting go of permanence makes way for clarity and peace. Life is a series of moments, each one valuable because it is fleeting.

May 13
Trusting the Process of Growth

Growth often feels slow and subtle, almost imperceptible. But it is happening, in every step and every breath. Trusting that process, even when progress seems distant, is essential. Each challenge faced, each small victory won, is part of a greater transformation.

There is no rush on the path to healing. The journey is just as important as the destination. With each moment comes an opportunity to learn, to grow, and to reflect. Growth may not always be visible, but it is always there. The process of growth is steady, sometimes silent, but always significant. Trust in the unfolding of the path, knowing that each step taken moves closer to wholeness.

May 14
The Freedom in Letting Go

Holding on too tightly to past hurts or future worries creates unnecessary tension. Freedom is found in letting go—in releasing expectations, fears, and regrets. Letting go doesn't mean giving up; it means releasing the hold that these things have on the heart and mind.

Letting go is a practice of acceptance. Accepting that control is not always possible, and that sometimes the best way forward is to allow things to be as they are. In this acceptance, freedom from suffering emerges.

Life becomes lighter when the grip on old narratives is loosened. Letting go is the key to moving forward with clarity and peace.

May 15
The Power of Mindful Attention

Attention is one of the most powerful tools in the recovery process. Wherever attention is directed, energy flows. Mindfulness teaches the value of placing attention on the present, rather than being distracted by worries or desires.

Mindful attention creates a sense of peace. It brings awareness to the moment and invites an openness to experience life as it is. By placing attention fully on what is happening right now, the mind finds calm and balance. Attention, when harnessed with mindfulness, becomes the gateway to deeper understanding and healing. It reveals the truth of the present and opens the heart to new possibilities.

May 16
Gratitude as a Daily Practice

Gratitude is a powerful practice that shifts focus from what's lacking to what's already present. In the practice of gratitude, life's small joys become more visible, and challenges seem less overwhelming. Gratitude changes perception, transforming ordinary moments into sources of peace.

Focusing on what's good doesn't mean ignoring struggles but embracing the full range of experiences with a heart open to appreciation. Each day offers something to be grateful for, even in the midst of difficulties.

Gratitude, when practiced daily, cultivates a deep sense of contentment and connection to the world. It is a quiet, powerful tool that nurtures inner peace.

May 17
Honoring the Present Moment

The present moment is the only true reality. The mind often drifts toward the past or the future, but the present is where life happens. Honoring the present moment brings clarity, grounding, and peace. It's in this moment that true healing begins.

Each breath, each heartbeat is a reminder of being alive. There is no need to rush toward the next moment or hold onto the last. Being fully present allows for a deeper connection to life, and with that connection, inner peace arises.

The present moment holds everything needed for contentment. By honoring it, a space of calm and joy is cultivated, no matter what else is happening.

May 18
Walking the Path of Compassion

Compassion, both for oneself and others, is the foundation of healing. It is easy to be harsh, critical, and unforgiving, but compassion opens the heart to understanding and forgiveness. Compassion allows for mistakes, understanding that they are part of the human experience.

Walking the path of compassion means recognizing the suffering of others while also being kind to oneself. Each step on this path strengthens the ability to relate to others with care and to accept one's own imperfections.

Compassion is the softening of the heart. It brings a sense of connection and belonging, both in the recovery journey and in everyday life.

May 19
Reconnecting with Inner Strength

There is a well of strength within, one that often goes untapped during moments of doubt. Reconnecting with that inner strength provides a sense of stability, even in the face of challenges. This strength is always there, waiting to be accessed.

Recovery isn't about never feeling weak or unsure; it's about remembering that strength is always present, even in the midst of struggle. It is not about overpowering challenges but about moving through them with resilience.

Reconnecting with inner strength reminds the spirit that there is always enough strength to face whatever comes, even when it seems impossible.

May 20
The Journey of Self-Acceptance

Self-acceptance is a lifelong journey, one that requires patience and understanding. It means embracing all parts of oneself—the strengths, the flaws, the successes, and the failures. True healing begins with accepting who one is, without judgment or shame.

Self-acceptance doesn't come overnight. It is nurtured through small acts of kindness toward oneself, through recognizing that everyone is a work in progress. Recovery is not about perfection but about growth, and that growth begins with acceptance.

In the journey of self-acceptance, the mind and heart find peace. It is the foundation for lasting healing, offering a space of compassion and understanding.

May 21
The Power of Silence

In the silence, the mind finds clarity. The constant chatter, distractions, and noise can cloud judgment and create unnecessary stress. But in the quiet moments, there is a chance to reflect, to listen, and to understand life's deeper truths.

Silence offers space for the heart to open, for emotions to settle, and for insight to arise. It's in these moments of stillness that true peace can be felt. The absence of external noise makes room for an inner calm that is often overshadowed by the busyness of life.

Embracing silence isn't about avoiding life; it's about creating a space for life to unfold with more clarity and intention.

May 22
Embracing the Unknown

Fear often arises from the unknown, from not knowing what's next or how things will turn out. But life is filled with uncertainty, and embracing the unknown is a key part of growth. Holding too tightly to what's familiar can prevent new opportunities from unfolding.

Each moment of uncertainty is also a moment of possibility. The unknown can be approached not with fear, but with curiosity and openness. Instead of dreading the unknown, welcoming it as part of life's journey opens the door to new experiences.

Embracing the unknown allows for a sense of freedom. Life doesn't need to be perfectly planned out to be fulfilling—it simply needs to be lived with an open heart.

May 23
Healing through Forgiveness

Forgiveness isn't about excusing harmful behavior; it's about releasing the hold that resentment and anger have on the heart. Carrying the weight of past hurts only creates more suffering, while forgiveness lightens the emotional load.

Letting go of grudges and offering forgiveness allows for healing. It's not about condoning what has happened, but about freeing the mind from the pain of holding on to negativity. Forgiveness is an act of self-compassion, as much as it is an act of compassion toward others.

Through forgiveness, space is created for peace to take root. It's a practice of healing, both for the one who forgives and the one who is forgiven.

May 24
Trusting the Timing of Life

Life has its own rhythm, its own timing. Often, the desire to rush or control outcomes leads to frustration. But trusting in the timing of life brings a sense of ease. Each moment unfolds as it should, even if it doesn't match expectations.

Patience allows for this trust to grow. In moments of waiting, growth happens in unseen ways. There's no need to force or push; life's natural rhythm will reveal itself in time. Trusting this process brings peace and alleviates the pressure to make things happen too quickly.

Everything comes in its own time. By trusting the process, there is room to enjoy the journey rather than anxiously anticipating the destination.

May 25
The Strength in Stillness

Stillness is often misunderstood as weakness, but in stillness, strength is found. When the mind is quiet, there's an opportunity to reconnect with inner reserves of resilience and courage. The constant need to act can sometimes mask the power of simply being.

Taking time for stillness doesn't mean avoiding responsibilities or challenges; it means approaching them with a clearer mind and a stronger heart. Stillness invites reflection, and through reflection, insight emerges.

Stillness is where inner strength grows. It's where the heart can rest and the mind can clear, offering a renewed sense of energy and purpose for whatever comes next.

May 26
Seeing with Clarity

Clarity doesn't always come easily. The mind is often clouded with judgments, assumptions, and distractions. But when clarity is found, it brings a sense of freedom. To see clearly is to see things as they are, without the fog of personal biases or emotional turbulence.

Clarity arises through mindfulness, through the practice of paying attention to the present moment without attachment. It is not about forcing understanding, but about allowing insight to arise naturally. With clarity, decisions become easier, and peace becomes more accessible.

Seeing with clarity brings a deeper connection to the truth. It clears away the confusion, leaving room for wisdom and compassion to guide the way.

May 27
The Practice of Patience

Patience is a practice that requires intentionality. It's easy to become frustrated when things don't happen on a desired timeline or when obstacles arise. But in moments of impatience, there's an opportunity to cultivate calm and understanding.

Patience isn't about passive waiting; it's about actively choosing to remain peaceful in the face of uncertainty or delay. Each moment of impatience is a chance to practice mindfulness, to breathe, and to let go of the need for control.

Patience allows for a more compassionate view of oneself and others. It's through patience that lasting change and healing can take root.

May 28
Accepting Imperfection

Perfection is an illusion, one that often leads to frustration and disappointment. In the pursuit of perfection, it's easy to overlook the beauty of imperfection—the small, human flaws that make life real and relatable.

Accepting imperfection doesn't mean giving up on growth or improvement; it means recognizing that perfection isn't necessary for worth or happiness. The more imperfections are embraced, the more life can be lived with a sense of freedom and authenticity.

In imperfection, there is grace. Accepting that nothing is flawless, including oneself, opens the door to deeper self-compassion and a more meaningful connection with others.

May 29

Grounding in the Present

The present moment is the only one that can be truly lived. Thoughts of the past or worries about the future often pull attention away from what's happening right now. Grounding in the present offers an anchor, a way to reconnect with what is real.

The mind can wander, but by gently bringing attention back to the breath, the sensations in the body, or the environment, a deeper sense of peace is cultivated. Grounding in the present allows for a fuller experience of life, one that is not overshadowed by regret or fear.

Grounding practices bring a sense of stability. In the present, there is clarity, calm, and the potential for growth.

May 30
The Balance Between Effort and Surrender

Effort is essential on the path to recovery, but so is surrender. There is a delicate balance between striving to improve and accepting what cannot be changed. Too much effort can lead to burnout, while too much surrender can lead to passivity.

Finding balance means knowing when to push forward and when to let go. It's a practice of tuning into what is needed in each moment. Some days require more effort, while others call for a gentle surrender to life's unfolding. The balance between effort and surrender creates harmony. It allows for growth without strain and peace without stagnation.

May 31
Reflecting on the Journey So Far

As the month comes to a close, it's a time to reflect on the journey so far. There have been challenges, moments of growth, and times of uncertainty. Each day has offered something new—a lesson, an insight, a chance for healing.

Reflection brings awareness to how far the path has been traveled, and how much has been learned. It's important to acknowledge both the progress made and the lessons still unfolding. This journey is ongoing, and each step is valuable.

Looking back with a sense of gratitude and forward with hope brings a sense of peace. The journey is one of constant discovery, with each day offering something new to learn.

JUNE

June 1
The Seed of Intention

Every action begins with an intention. Whether conscious or unconscious, intention drives decisions, words, and behavior. Taking time to set clear intentions can shape the direction of each day, fostering mindfulness and purpose in recovery.

An intention can be simple: a commitment to stay present, to be kind, or to face challenges with courage. This seed of intention, when planted in the mind, guides thoughts and actions, allowing them to align with deeper values and aspirations.

With a clear intention, each moment of the day becomes an opportunity for growth. The seed, once planted, begins to take root, shaping how life unfolds with greater clarity and purpose.

June 2
The Weight of Expectations

Expectations often lead to disappointment. Holding onto rigid ideas of how things should be creates unnecessary stress. Instead of allowing life to unfold naturally, there's a tendency to measure everything against preconceived outcomes.

Letting go of expectations brings a sense of relief. It opens up space for appreciation of what is, rather than frustration over what isn't. When expectations are loosened, life becomes more fluid, more adaptable to whatever comes.

Releasing the weight of expectations lightens the mind. It allows for a greater sense of freedom and invites a deeper acceptance of the present moment, no matter how it appears.

June 3
The Strength in Vulnerability

Vulnerability is often seen as a weakness, but it's one of the greatest sources of strength. Opening up, whether to oneself or others, requires courage. It's in these moments of honesty and openness that true healing begins.

To admit vulnerability is to recognize that being human means experiencing hurt, confusion, and fear. It's through these emotions that deeper growth can happen. There's no need to pretend to be invulnerable, as this only builds barriers to connection and healing.

Embracing vulnerability allows for a fuller, more authentic life. In admitting weakness, strength is found, and in acknowledging wounds, the process of healing can truly begin.

June 4
The Practice of Letting Go

Holding onto past pain, mistakes, or regrets creates emotional heaviness. Letting go doesn't mean forgetting or dismissing what has happened—it means releasing the emotional grip it has on the present.

Letting go is a practice, one that requires patience and compassion. It's about recognizing that clinging to past hurt only deepens suffering. By loosening the grip on these experiences, space is made for new growth and healing.

The act of letting go brings lightness. It frees the heart and mind from burdens that no longer serve, allowing for a more peaceful and present life.

June 5
The Value of Simplicity

In a world that often encourages complexity, simplicity is a gift. Overcomplicating life's problems can make challenges seem insurmountable, but stripping things down to their essence offers clarity and relief.

Simplicity doesn't mean avoiding depth. It's about focusing on what truly matters and letting go of distractions that pull energy away from the present. In recovery, simplicity can be a guiding principle, helping to keep the mind and heart clear.

By embracing simplicity, life becomes less cluttered. Decisions become easier, emotions more balanced, and there is space to focus on what's truly important: healing, growth, and inner peace.

June 6
Finding Comfort in the Uncomfortable

Growth doesn't always come from comfort. In fact, it's often in the most uncomfortable moments that the greatest progress is made. Discomfort forces a deeper look within, revealing areas of life that need attention and change.

Finding comfort in the uncomfortable means accepting that not all growth feels good in the moment. It's about trusting the process, even when it feels challenging or uncertain. There's strength in sitting with discomfort, knowing it won't last forever.

Embracing discomfort as part of the journey makes it less threatening. It becomes a stepping stone toward deeper understanding and transformation, rather than something to be feared or avoided.

June 7
The Power of Gratitude

Gratitude is a transformative practice. When the mind is filled with gratitude, it shifts focus from what is lacking to what is present. Gratitude doesn't erase life's difficulties, but it changes the way those difficulties are experienced.

Recognizing the small, everyday things to be grateful for builds resilience. Gratitude creates a mindset that is more open to the present, less burdened by stress or anxiety. It's a reminder that even in hard times, there is always something to appreciate.

Gratitude brings light into dark places. It opens the heart, making room for joy and peace, even in the midst of life's challenges.

June 8
The Quiet Strength of Patience

Patience is often seen as passive, but it's an active and powerful practice. It takes strength to wait, to allow things to unfold in their own time without forcing outcomes. Patience cultivates resilience and teaches that not everything needs to be rushed.

In recovery, patience is essential. Progress doesn't always come quickly, and setbacks may happen along the way. But with patience, each step is recognized as valuable, no matter how small.

Patience allows for a deeper connection to the present moment. It eases the mind, bringing peace to situations that might otherwise create frustration or anxiety.

June 9
The Practice of Self-Compassion

Self-compassion is the foundation for healing. It's easy to be harsh with oneself, to focus on mistakes or shortcomings. But self-compassion brings a gentleness that is necessary for recovery.

Offering compassion to oneself means recognizing that everyone struggles, and that it's okay to stumble. It's about treating oneself with the same kindness and understanding that would be offered to a close friend.

Through self-compassion, healing becomes possible. It allows for growth without judgment and offers the space to learn and move forward with a softer, more loving heart.

June 10
Trusting the Process of Change

Change is inevitable, but it's often met with resistance. There's comfort in what's known, even if it no longer serves. Trusting the process of change means letting go of the need to control every outcome and accepting that change brings new opportunities for growth.

Each phase of change, no matter how uncomfortable, offers something valuable. It may not be clear in the moment, but with time, the purpose behind the change often reveals itself. Trusting in the process allows for more ease and less resistance.

Change is part of life's natural rhythm. Embracing it opens the door to new possibilities and a deeper sense of peace.

June 11
The Beauty of Imperfection

Perfection is a myth that creates unnecessary pressure. Chasing perfection often leads to feelings of failure or inadequacy, yet life, in all its messiness, is perfect in its own way. Embracing imperfections allows for more compassion and acceptance of the self and others.

The beauty of imperfection lies in its honesty. Life doesn't follow a straight line, and neither does the path of recovery. There will be mistakes, setbacks, and challenges, but these don't define the journey. Instead, they offer opportunities to learn and grow.

Accepting imperfection as a natural part of life brings peace. It shifts the focus from trying to control everything to finding joy in the unpredictable, ever-changing nature of the present moment.

June 12
The Freedom of Forgiveness

Forgiveness is often seen as a gift to others, but in truth, it's a gift to oneself. Holding onto anger, resentment, or guilt weighs down the heart and mind. Forgiveness doesn't excuse harmful behavior, but it frees the one who forgives from the pain of carrying past wounds.

Forgiveness requires strength and vulnerability. It's not about forgetting or condoning what has happened but about releasing the emotional grip it has on the present. Forgiveness brings freedom, allowing for peace to take the place of bitterness.

The act of forgiveness opens the door to healing. It lightens the load, making space for new possibilities and a more compassionate connection with the world.

June 13
The Quiet Power of Reflection

Reflection is a powerful tool for growth. Taking time to look inward, to examine thoughts, feelings, and experiences, creates space for deeper understanding. Reflection isn't about judging or criticizing; it's about observing with curiosity and openness.

In the stillness of reflection, patterns emerge. It becomes clear where growth is happening and where there's still work to be done. Reflection allows for insight, guiding decisions and actions with greater clarity.

By regularly reflecting on the journey, progress becomes more visible. The quiet power of reflection lies in its ability to reveal the truth of the present moment, offering a compass for the road ahead.

June 14
The Path of Compassion

Compassion is at the heart of healing. It's not just about kindness toward others but also about extending that same kindness to oneself. Compassion softens the heart, allowing for deeper connection and understanding.

Walking the path of compassion requires patience and practice. It means choosing to respond with care, even in difficult situations, and recognizing that everyone is struggling in their own way. Compassion is not weakness; it is a profound strength that nurtures growth. As compassion grows, so does peace. The more the heart opens to the suffering of others, the more it heals its own pain, creating a ripple effect of love and understanding that touches everyone.

June 15
The Balance of Effort and Surrender

In life, there is a delicate balance between effort and surrender. Effort is necessary to move forward, to make progress in recovery, but there comes a point when surrender is equally important. Holding too tightly to control can create unnecessary struggle.

Surrender isn't giving up; it's letting go of the need to control every outcome. It's trusting that, after putting in the effort, life will unfold as it should. This balance creates a sense of peace, allowing for both action and acceptance.

Finding balance between effort and surrender brings ease to the process of recovery. It allows for movement without force, growth without pressure, and a more harmonious relationship with life as it is.

June 16
The Gift of Presence

Being present is one of the greatest gifts that can be offered—to oneself, to others, and to the world. The present moment is where life happens, where healing and connection take place. Yet, it's easy to get lost in thoughts of the past or worries about the future.

The gift of presence requires intention. It means consciously bringing attention to what is happening right now, without judgment or distraction. This simple practice transforms ordinary moments into opportunities for mindfulness, connection, and growth.

Presence brings peace. It slows down the mind, allowing for greater clarity and a deeper appreciation of life's small, beautiful moments.

June 17
The Courage to Begin Again

Every day offers the chance to begin again. Recovery is not a linear path, and there will be moments of struggle or setback. But with each new day comes the opportunity to start fresh, to take one more step toward healing.

Beginning again requires courage. It means facing fears and doubts and moving forward despite them. It's about accepting that mistakes happen but not letting them define the future.

There is great strength in beginning again. It's a reminder that growth is always possible, no matter how many times the journey has been interrupted. Each new beginning is a step toward greater peace and understanding.

June 18
The Wisdom of Silence

Silence holds great wisdom. In a world filled with constant noise and distraction, the ability to sit in silence allows for deeper listening—both to the self and to the world around. Silence is where truth often emerges, free from the clutter of thoughts and external influence.

Sitting in silence isn't about avoiding life's challenges; it's about creating space to observe them without judgment. In the stillness, emotions and thoughts are seen more clearly, allowing for greater understanding and insight.

Silence is a teacher. It shows that not everything needs to be fixed or solved immediately. Sometimes, simply sitting with what is can bring more clarity and peace than any amount of action or words.

June 19
The Path of Humility

Humility is often misunderstood as weakness, but it is a source of great strength. True humility is about recognizing one's own limitations while remaining open to learning and growth. It's about acknowledging that no one has all the answers and that everyone is on a journey.

Walking the path of humility creates space for deeper connection with others. It allows for more compassion and understanding, as there is no need to prove superiority or control. Humility makes way for genuine relationships and meaningful progress in recovery.

With humility comes peace. It frees the mind from the burden of ego, allowing for greater openness and acceptance of life as it unfolds.

June 20
The Power of Patience

Patience is a powerful practice in recovery. Progress doesn't always come quickly, and the mind can become restless when things don't move at the desired pace. But patience creates space for growth to happen in its own time.

Patience teaches that not everything needs to be rushed. It shows that the process of healing is just as important as the outcome. With patience, there is more room for compassion, both toward oneself and others.

Patience brings peace to the journey. It allows for a more gentle, accepting approach to recovery, where each step is valued for what it is, without the need for haste or perfection.

June 21
The Strength in Vulnerability

Vulnerability is often seen as a weakness, but in truth, it takes great strength to be open and honest about one's struggles. Recovery requires vulnerability, whether it's admitting mistakes, asking for help, or simply acknowledging the emotions that arise.

The act of being vulnerable creates deeper connections with others and allows for more authentic healing. It breaks down the barriers of isolation and fear, making way for trust and understanding. There is power in showing up as one truly is, without the need for pretense. Vulnerability brings freedom. It strips away the layers of defense, allowing for more genuine experiences, both in recovery and in everyday life. By embracing vulnerability, there is space for growth, connection, and true healing.

June 22
The Practice of Mindful Action

Mindful action means moving through the world with awareness. It's not just about doing things; it's about doing them with presence and intention. Whether it's something as simple as walking or as complex as making a life decision, mindful action brings clarity and focus.

The practice of mindful action shifts the focus from achieving results to fully engaging with the process. This doesn't mean that outcomes don't matter, but it means that the way something is done becomes just as important as what is done.

Mindful action creates balance. It transforms even the most mundane tasks into opportunities for mindfulness and self-awareness, bringing peace and purpose to every moment of the day.

June 23
The Art of Letting Go

Letting go is a key part of recovery. It's not just about letting go of harmful behaviors or substances; it's also about releasing the need to control every outcome. Holding on too tightly creates tension, while letting go creates space for peace and healing.

Letting go doesn't mean giving up. It means trusting that life will unfold as it's meant to, without forcing or resisting. It's about releasing attachment to what can't be controlled and focusing instead on what can be changed.

There is freedom in letting go. It allows for more openness, more ease, and more acceptance of life as it is, rather than how it "should" be. This practice brings peace to the mind and heart, creating space for deeper healing.

June 24
The Gift of Gratitude

Gratitude is a simple but profound practice. In recovery, it's easy to focus on what's lacking or what's difficult, but shifting the focus to what is already present—what is good—can change everything. Gratitude brings perspective and creates a sense of abundance, even in challenging times.

The gift of gratitude is that it transforms the ordinary into something extraordinary. By recognizing the blessings in each day, no matter how small, the mind is trained to see the good rather than fixate on the negative. Gratitude opens the heart. It brings joy, even in the midst of struggle, and cultivates a deeper connection with life itself. The practice of gratitude strengthens the spirit and supports the journey of recovery.

June 25
The Patience to Heal

Healing takes time, and the process is not always linear. Patience is required to navigate the ups and downs of recovery, allowing space for setbacks without falling into discouragement. Healing is not about perfection; it's about progress.

The patience to heal means accepting that growth happens at its own pace. It's about trusting that even when things feel stagnant or difficult, healing is still taking place. Patience allows for more compassion toward oneself, reducing the pressure to "get it right."

With patience comes peace. The journey of recovery becomes less about reaching a destination and more about appreciating each step along the way, no matter how long it takes.

June 26
The Strength of Community

Recovery is not something to be done alone. The strength of community is one of the greatest supports in the journey toward healing. Whether through formal groups or personal connections, being part of a community provides a sense of belonging and understanding.

Community offers accountability, encouragement, and shared wisdom. It reminds that no one has to walk this path by themselves. The experiences of others can illuminate one's own struggles, offering new perspectives and insights.

The strength of community lies in its collective power. Together, individuals can lift each other up, providing support during times of need and celebrating growth along the way.

June 27
The Simplicity of Breath

The breath is a powerful anchor in recovery. In moments of stress, anxiety, or craving, simply returning attention to the breath can create a sense of calm. It's always there, a steady rhythm that connects the body and mind to the present moment.

Breathing mindfully brings the mind back to stillness. It interrupts the spiral of thoughts and emotions that can overwhelm. Focusing on the breath is a simple but profound practice that nurtures mindfulness and inner peace.

The simplicity of breath is its greatest strength. No matter where one is or what is happening, the breath is always accessible. It offers a direct path to calm, clarity, and grounding.

June 28
The Power of Self-Acceptance

Self-acceptance is a cornerstone of recovery. It's about recognizing that while there is always room for growth, the present self is worthy of love and respect. Recovery can bring up feelings of shame or inadequacy, but self-acceptance counters these with kindness.

The power of self-acceptance lies in its ability to heal wounds of the past. By accepting oneself fully, without judgment or comparison, the mind becomes more peaceful, and the path forward becomes clearer.

True self-acceptance brings freedom. It removes the need for constant self-criticism, replacing it with compassion and understanding. This practice is a powerful tool for healing and growth in recovery.

June 29
The Importance of Boundaries

Boundaries are essential in recovery. They protect emotional, mental, and physical well-being, creating a space where healing can happen without being overwhelmed by outside forces. Setting and maintaining boundaries requires strength and clarity.

Healthy boundaries are not about isolation or control but about honoring one's own needs and limits. They create space for more authentic relationships and prevent burnout or resentment.

Boundaries bring balance. By respecting personal limits, it's possible to engage with others in a more mindful and present way, ensuring that recovery remains the top priority without sacrificing connection.

June 30
The Courage to Change

Change is at the heart of recovery. It requires courage to leave behind old patterns, behaviors, and ways of thinking. But change is also where growth happens. Every step taken toward healing is an act of bravery.

The courage to change doesn't mean that change will be easy or straightforward. It means being willing to face discomfort, uncertainty, and fear in order to move forward. It's about trusting the process, even when the outcome is unclear.

With courage comes transformation. The willingness to change, to grow, and to heal opens the door to a new way of living—one that is rooted in peace, balance, and deeper understanding.

J
U
L
Y

July 1
The Wisdom of Humility

Humility is often misunderstood as weakness, but in truth, it is a great strength. It's about acknowledging limitations, being open to learning, and recognizing that growth comes from admitting what is not known. In recovery, humility allows for progress without the need for perfection.

Humility fosters an attitude of openness. It invites the willingness to listen, to be guided, and to accept that others may hold valuable insights. When humility is practiced, pride and ego begin to dissolve, making room for genuine connection with oneself and others.

In humility, there is peace. It removes the burden of having to always be right or in control. Instead, it allows for the flow of life to unfold naturally, with the understanding that each moment offers a lesson worth embracing.

July 2
The Practice of Daily Recommitment

Each day in recovery is a chance to recommit to the journey. No matter what happened the day before, the present offers a new opportunity to choose healing and growth. Recommitment is not about perfection; it's about persistence and resilience.

By committing daily, the practice of recovery becomes more about consistency than intensity. There is no need to achieve everything at once; rather, progress is made through small, deliberate actions. This process teaches patience and encourages long-term change.

Daily recommitment brings strength. It reinforces the intention to live mindfully and with purpose, focusing on each step along the path rather than being overwhelmed by the entirety of the journey.

July 3
The Gift of Forgiveness

Forgiveness, whether of oneself or others, is a powerful tool for healing. It releases the weight of resentment, guilt, and anger, creating space for peace and renewal. Forgiveness is not about condoning harm but about freeing the heart from its grip.

The process of forgiveness begins within. Before others can be forgiven, it's essential to offer forgiveness to oneself. Recovery often involves facing past mistakes, and without self-forgiveness, true healing can be hindered.

Forgiveness restores balance. It allows for the past to be acknowledged without being held captive by it. Through forgiveness, the mind is liberated, and the path toward healing becomes clearer and more compassionate.

July 4
The Joy in Small Victories

Recovery is made up of countless small victories. Each step forward, no matter how minor it seems, is a reason to celebrate. These victories build momentum, providing the strength and motivation to continue the journey toward healing.

Acknowledging small victories shifts the focus from what remains undone to what has already been achieved. It cultivates gratitude for progress, reinforcing the belief that change is not only possible but is happening, even in subtle ways.

In celebrating these moments, joy is found. The journey of recovery becomes less daunting when it's filled with small celebrations along the way. These victories remind that each step forward matters.

July 5
The Power of Intention

Intentions guide actions. In recovery, setting a clear intention can provide direction and purpose, even during challenging times. Intentions are less about what needs to be done and more about how to approach each day with mindfulness and awareness.

The power of intention lies in its ability to shift focus from external outcomes to internal states. It's not about controlling everything but about aligning with the core values and goals that support healing. Intentions offer clarity and remind what truly matters.

With intention, each day becomes more purposeful. It's not about perfection or rigid control, but about moving through the world with awareness and compassion, staying true to the path of recovery.

July 6
The Calm in Accepting What Is

Acceptance is a cornerstone of peace. It doesn't mean giving up or resigning oneself to circumstances but recognizing what is beyond control and choosing to make peace with it. In recovery, acceptance creates space for healing without the need to resist or fight against reality.

The calm in acceptance comes from releasing the need to change things that cannot be changed. It offers freedom from the mental and emotional turmoil that comes from wishing things were different. Instead, it invites an embrace of what is, with all its imperfections.

Acceptance is a powerful tool for inner peace. By letting go of the struggle to control everything, there is more energy available to focus on what truly matters—healing, growth, and living with purpose.

July 7
The Importance of Honesty

Honesty is the foundation of recovery. Without it, progress can be hindered, as truth is what leads to real change. Being honest, especially with oneself, is not always easy, but it is essential for growth and healing.

Honesty creates clarity. It strips away denial, rationalizations, and excuses, allowing for a deeper understanding of oneself and the journey. With honesty comes the ability to see things as they truly are, rather than as they are wished to be.

In honesty, there is strength. It builds integrity and trust, both within oneself and in relationships with others. The willingness to be truthful, even when it's difficult, opens the door to deeper healing and more authentic connections.

July 8
The Compassionate Heart

Compassion, both for oneself and others, is a vital part of the recovery process. It softens the edges of judgment and harsh self-criticism, replacing them with kindness and understanding. Compassion allows for mistakes without the need for punishment.

The compassionate heart sees struggle without condemnation. It offers support and patience, recognizing that recovery is not linear and that setbacks are a natural part of the process. Compassion helps navigate these moments with gentleness, rather than frustration or anger.

Compassion nurtures healing. It reminds that kindness, rather than harshness, is what encourages growth. By practicing compassion, both inwardly and outwardly, the journey of recovery becomes one of grace and understanding.

July 9
The Quiet Strength of Persistence

Persistence is a quiet but powerful force in recovery. It's not always about grand gestures or breakthroughs but about the steady, consistent effort to keep moving forward, even when progress feels slow or invisible.

The quiet strength of persistence is that it builds resilience. Each small effort, each choice to stay on the path, reinforces the commitment to healing. Persistence doesn't require perfection; it simply asks for continued effort, even in the face of challenges.

Persistence leads to transformation. Over time, the small, consistent steps taken toward recovery add up, creating lasting change. The journey may not always be easy, but with persistence, it is always moving forward.

July 10
The Practice of Self-Compassion

Self-compassion is about treating oneself with the same kindness and understanding that would be extended to a friend. It's about acknowledging the difficulties faced in recovery without judgment or harshness. Self-compassion creates space for healing.

The practice of self-compassion begins by recognizing that everyone makes mistakes, and that struggle is part of being human. It's not about excusing harmful behavior but about responding to it with patience and care, rather than shame.

With self-compassion, recovery becomes more sustainable. It allows for growth without the need for perfection, creating a more nurturing and supportive environment for healing. The journey is made lighter when walked with compassion toward oneself.

July 11
The Healing Power of Gratitude

Gratitude has the power to transform even the most challenging situations. In recovery, it can be easy to focus on the difficulties, but when gratitude is practiced, a shift in perspective occurs. Gratitude doesn't mean ignoring struggles, but it allows for the recognition of what is still good.

Gratitude opens the heart and mind to the present moment. It invites reflection on the small blessings that often go unnoticed—things like the support of a friend, a moment of peace, or the strength to continue on the journey. These moments, when appreciated, bring lightness to the path.

Practicing gratitude daily fosters resilience. It acts as a reminder that even in the midst of struggle, there is always something to be thankful for. Gratitude nurtures a sense of peace and strengthens the commitment to healing.

July 12
Embracing Impermanence

Everything is constantly changing, whether it is recognized or not. In recovery, embracing the truth of impermanence can be freeing. It serves as a reminder that both the struggles and the successes are temporary, always evolving.

Impermanence teaches flexibility and non-attachment. When it is understood that nothing stays the same, there is less need to cling tightly to outcomes, people, or experiences. This openness to change creates space for growth, healing, and acceptance of the present moment.

The beauty of impermanence lies in its potential for renewal. No matter how difficult a moment may feel, it will pass. And with its passing, there is the possibility for something new—another step forward, another chance to grow.

July 13
The Strength in Vulnerability

Vulnerability is often seen as a weakness, but in recovery, it is a source of immense strength. Allowing oneself to be open, to admit to fears, mistakes, and uncertainties, takes great courage. Vulnerability is not about being weak; it is about being honest and real.

Through vulnerability, true connection becomes possible. It's in sharing struggles that understanding and support can be found. When the walls of pretense are dropped, healing deepens, as the need to maintain a façade is let go. Strength grows through vulnerability. By facing fears and acknowledging the truth, inner strength is built, creating a solid foundation for continued growth. Vulnerability invites authenticity, which is the heart of real recovery.

July 14
Cultivating Patience with the Process

Recovery is a long and sometimes unpredictable journey. Patience is essential in allowing the process to unfold at its own pace. There may be setbacks, frustrations, and moments of doubt, but patience nurtures the understanding that all things take time.

Patience softens the urge to rush. It reminds that healing is not linear, nor does it happen overnight. With patience, there is more room for reflection, self-care, and the acknowledgment that progress is being made, even when it feels slow.

Patience is a form of trust. It's trusting that the path being walked, though difficult at times, is leading somewhere meaningful. With patience, the journey of recovery becomes more sustainable and less burdened by the pressure to achieve immediate results.

July 15
Letting Go of Control

Recovery often highlights the desire to control everything—outcomes, feelings, and even other people. But true peace comes from letting go of this need for control. It's about accepting that not everything can be controlled, and that's okay.

Letting go of control doesn't mean giving up. Instead, it means shifting focus from controlling external circumstances to managing internal reactions. By releasing the need to control everything, there is more space to respond mindfully to what life presents.

In letting go, there is freedom. It allows for the unexpected and the unknown to unfold without resistance. It creates space for acceptance, for the practice of presence, and for the realization that control is often an illusion.

July 16
The Value of Stillness

In a fast-paced world, stillness can feel like an impossible luxury, yet it is in stillness that clarity and peace are found. Stillness isn't just about being physically quiet; it's about creating moments of internal calm where thoughts can settle and insights can emerge. Stillness invites reflection. It offers the chance to pause, breathe, and take stock of what's happening in both the external world and the internal landscape. In recovery, stillness allows for deeper self-awareness and a reconnection with the intentions behind the journey.

The value of stillness is that it provides balance. It helps to counteract the chaos and busyness of life, reminding that sometimes, doing nothing is exactly what is needed for healing and growth.

July 17
Trusting the Journey

Trust is a crucial element in recovery, yet it can be difficult to cultivate, especially after past disappointments or challenges. Trusting the journey doesn't mean knowing exactly where it leads but having faith in the process itself.

Trusting the journey involves letting go of expectations. It's about believing that the path being walked is leading toward healing, even if the steps aren't always clear. Trust allows for surrender, which in turn reduces anxiety and fear about the future.

Trust is what sustains the journey. By trusting that each step, no matter how small, is part of a larger picture, recovery becomes less about reaching a specific destination and more about embracing the process as it unfolds.

July 18
The Gift of Presence

Being present is one of the greatest gifts that can be offered, both to oneself and others. In recovery, the practice of presence means fully engaging with the current moment, without distraction or judgment. It's about being here, now.

Presence creates connection. When fully present, there is a deeper awareness of thoughts, emotions, and surroundings. It opens the heart and mind to the richness of life, even in its simplest moments. This awareness strengthens the connection to oneself and to the recovery journey.

The gift of presence brings clarity. It helps to cut through the noise of past regrets and future anxieties, grounding attention in what is happening now. Through presence, life becomes more vibrant, and the practice of mindfulness deepens.

July 19
The Courage to Begin Again

Recovery is not about perfection, and often it involves starting over, sometimes more than once. Having the courage to begin again is one of the most important aspects of the journey. Each new beginning offers the opportunity for renewed commitment and growth.

Beginning again requires humility. It means admitting when things have gone off course and having the strength to try again, without shame or self-judgment. Each time the decision is made to continue, the foundation of recovery becomes stronger.

The courage to begin again is the essence of resilience. No matter how many times a fall happens, the choice to rise again is what defines the journey. With each new beginning, healing deepens and the path forward becomes clearer.

July 20
The Quiet Grace of Simplicity

Simplicity is a quiet grace that brings peace and clarity. In recovery, simplicity can mean letting go of unnecessary complications—whether in actions, thoughts, or emotions. It's about finding joy in the simple, steady rhythm of life.

Simplicity invites focus. By reducing distractions and unnecessary clutter, it becomes easier to concentrate on what truly matters—healing, mindfulness, and presence. The more simplicity is embraced, the more space there is for peace to flourish.

In simplicity, life feels lighter. The weight of overcomplication is lifted, leaving room for deeper awareness and appreciation. Simplicity offers a return to basics, where the most important things are clear and accessible.

July 21
Honoring Personal Boundaries

In recovery, learning to establish and honor personal boundaries is crucial for healing. Boundaries are not about shutting others out but about protecting one's well-being. They create a safe space in which growth can happen without external pressures or harmful influences. Setting boundaries takes courage and self-awareness. It requires knowing what is acceptable and what is not, then acting in alignment with that understanding. By honoring these limits, trust in oneself grows, and the ability to engage with others from a place of authenticity is strengthened.

Healthy boundaries create freedom. They allow for a sense of autonomy and clarity, reducing feelings of overwhelm and fostering respect in relationships. By respecting personal boundaries, recovery becomes more grounded and sustainable.

July 22
The Power of Forgiveness

Forgiveness is often misunderstood as condoning wrongdoing, but in truth, it's a powerful tool for healing. In recovery, forgiveness means letting go of the anger, resentment, and blame that keep wounds open. It's about releasing the hold that past harm has over the present.

Forgiveness is a process. It doesn't happen overnight and may need to be revisited over time. Yet, with each step toward forgiveness—whether for oneself or others—the weight of the past lightens. It allows for a sense of peace to replace the lingering pain.

True forgiveness offers freedom. It frees the heart from the bitterness that holds it back and creates space for healing and compassion. In letting go, there is an opening to move forward without the burden of what once was.

July 23
Embracing Humility

Humility is not about being small or insignificant; it's about recognizing one's place in the larger flow of life. In recovery, humility teaches the importance of accepting limitations and understanding that no one is above the need for help, healing, or support.

Humility fosters openness. When there is humility, the walls of ego and defensiveness fall away. It becomes easier to admit when help is needed, to ask questions, and to listen deeply to the wisdom of others. This openness invites connection and growth.

True humility brings peace. It's the realization that life is a shared experience, and there is no need to carry the weight of the world alone. Humility dissolves the need for perfection, allowing room for acceptance and grace.

July 24
The Lightness of Letting Go

Letting go is one of the most challenging and liberating aspects of recovery. Whether it's letting go of past mistakes, unfulfilled expectations, or the need for control, the process allows space for healing and renewal. Letting go doesn't mean forgetting; it means releasing the hold these things have on the present.

Letting go brings lightness. It removes the heavy burden of what cannot be changed or controlled. The more one releases attachment to past or future outcomes, the more there is space to focus on the present, where real growth happens.

In the lightness of letting go, there is freedom. It's an invitation to trust the process of life without needing to grip tightly to specific outcomes. Letting go is an act of faith, and in that faith, there is room for new possibilities to emerge.

July 25
The Healing Power of Nature

Nature has an unparalleled ability to restore balance. Whether it's a walk in the woods, listening to the sound of the ocean, or simply observing the changing sky, nature provides a space for healing. In recovery, reconnecting with nature helps to ground the body and quiet the mind.

Being in nature invites presence. The simplicity of natural rhythms—the rising sun, the steady growth of trees, the flow of rivers—reminds us that healing is a process that unfolds in its own time. Nature offers the chance to pause and reconnect with what is most essential.

Nature's healing power is in its stillness and constancy. It's a reminder that no matter how turbulent life may feel, there is always a calm center available. By attuning to the rhythms of the natural world, recovery is supported with a sense of peace and groundedness.

July 26
Cultivating Self-Compassion

Self-compassion is the foundation of healing. In recovery, the ability to be kind to oneself during difficult moments creates a safe space for growth. Self-compassion acknowledges the reality of struggle while offering understanding and gentleness instead of judgment.

Self-compassion allows for imperfection. It's the practice of treating oneself with the same kindness and care that would be extended to a loved one. This gentleness reduces the harshness of self-criticism, replacing it with encouragement and patience.

The more self-compassion is practiced, the deeper the healing. It fosters resilience by creating a nurturing inner environment where mistakes are seen as part of the process, not as failures. Through self-compassion, there is room for growth and acceptance.

July 27
The Strength of Community

Recovery is rarely a solo journey. The strength of community lies in the shared experiences, support, and wisdom of others. In a community, the journey becomes less isolating, and the collective strength of the group helps carry individuals through difficult times.

Community offers connection. It reminds that no one is alone in their struggles. Whether through group meetings, friendships, or support networks, being part of a community creates a sense of belonging and understanding that is essential to healing.

The strength of community is in its shared commitment to growth. Together, challenges are faced, victories are celebrated, and the journey toward recovery is supported. In community, there is strength, and in that strength, healing flourishes.

July 28
Accepting What Cannot Be Changed

One of the hardest lessons in recovery is accepting what cannot be changed. Whether it's the past, other people's actions, or certain outcomes, there are things in life that are beyond control. Acceptance is not resignation; it's a peaceful acknowledgment of reality.

Acceptance brings clarity. When there is a willingness to stop fighting against what cannot be changed, energy is freed to focus on what can be influenced—the present moment. Acceptance creates space for more mindful and effective action.

In accepting what cannot be changed, there is freedom. It's the release of resistance that allows for peace, even in the face of difficulty. Through acceptance, there is a greater sense of calm and the ability to move forward with grace.

July 29
The Wisdom of Patience

Patience is not passive; it is an active form of wisdom. In recovery, patience allows for the recognition that healing takes time. There is no rush, no finish line. Patience nurtures the understanding that every step, no matter how small, is part of the journey.

Patience reduces frustration. It reminds that setbacks and slow progress are natural parts of growth. When there is patience, there is less need to force outcomes, and more space is created for things to unfold naturally, in their own time.

The wisdom of patience is in its gentleness. It offers a compassionate approach to oneself and to others, recognizing that everyone's path is unique. Through patience, peace is found, and the process of recovery becomes more sustainable.

July 30
The Quiet Strength of Perseverance

Perseverance is the quiet strength that keeps one moving forward, even in the face of challenges. It's not about pushing through with force but about continuing to take steps, however small, toward healing. Perseverance is the steady commitment to growth.

Perseverance is fueled by hope. It's the belief that change is possible and that each effort, no matter how difficult, is moving in the right direction. With perseverance, the focus shifts from immediate results to the long-term vision of recovery.

The quiet strength of perseverance lies in its consistency. By continuing to show up for the work of healing, progress is made. Perseverance builds resilience, and with each step forward, the path of recovery becomes more clear and certain.

July 31
Celebrating Progress

In recovery, it's important to take time to celebrate progress. This doesn't mean only celebrating the big milestones, but also acknowledging the small victories—the moments of insight, the days of peace, the steps taken toward healing.

Celebrating progress nurtures gratitude. It allows for a reflection on how far the journey has come, even if it still feels like there's a long way to go. Each moment of progress, no matter how small, is worth recognizing and appreciating.

The celebration of progress creates momentum. It fosters a positive outlook and strengthens the commitment to continue the work of recovery. By celebrating the journey, not just the destination, healing becomes a more joyful and fulfilling process.

A
U
G
U
S
T

August 1
The Inevitability of Change

Change is one of the few constants in life. In recovery, change is not only inevitable but necessary for growth and transformation. Whether it's a shift in mindset, behavior, or environment, the willingness to embrace change is key to healing.

Change often brings discomfort. The mind clings to what is familiar, even if it's harmful, out of fear of the unknown. Yet, when there is acceptance of change, the possibility of new beginnings and a healthier way of living opens up.

Growth is found through change. By leaning into it, rather than resisting, the potential for transformation becomes greater. Change allows space for new opportunities, insights, and a deeper connection to the recovery journey.

August 2
Letting Go of Old Identities

Part of the recovery process involves shedding old identities. The roles that were played, the labels that were given or taken on during addiction, often no longer fit. Letting go of these identities is a necessary step in creating space for new, healthier ways of being.

Letting go of an old identity can be unsettling. It often feels like stepping into a void where the familiar safety net has been removed. But this space is where true freedom resides—the freedom to redefine who one is without the constraints of the past.

In recovery, the release of old identities opens the door to becoming more authentic. It's not about reinventing oneself but returning to a more honest and true version. This shedding of layers allows for growth and the discovery of a deeper, more meaningful self.

August 3
Facing Fears Head-On

Fear can be a powerful force in life, holding back progress and maintaining the status quo. In recovery, it's important to confront these fears—whether they're fears of failure, change, or the unknown. Facing fears head-on is how growth happens.

Fear has a way of magnifying itself when left unchecked. It often presents worst-case scenarios or exaggerated outcomes. By acknowledging fear and moving through it with courage, its grip loosens, and the path forward becomes clearer.

Courage is not the absence of fear but the decision to move forward despite it. Every step taken in the face of fear builds resilience and confidence. In facing fears, the barriers to growth and recovery begin to dissolve.

August 4
Trusting the Process of Healing

Healing is a process, and it doesn't always follow a linear path. In recovery, there will be ups and downs, moments of progress, and setbacks. Trusting the process means having faith that each step, no matter how difficult, is part of the journey toward healing.

The mind often wants quick fixes and immediate results, but true healing takes time. It unfolds in its own way, at its own pace. Trusting the process means letting go of the need for control and allowing space for growth to happen naturally.

When trust is placed in the process, there is less resistance. The more one surrenders to the flow of recovery, the easier it becomes to navigate its twists and turns. Healing is not a destination; it's a journey, and trusting that journey makes it more fulfilling.

August 5

Resilience in the Face of Adversity

Resilience is the ability to bounce back after setbacks. In recovery, adversity is often encountered, whether it's in the form of external challenges or internal struggles. Resilience is what keeps one moving forward, even in the toughest moments.

Adversity tests strength. It's through these tests that resilience is built, as each challenge becomes an opportunity for growth. The key is to see adversity not as a failure but as part of the process of becoming stronger.

Resilience is nurtured by persistence. By continuing to show up, even when it feels difficult or uncomfortable, resilience grows. With each step taken, no matter how small, the ability to handle future challenges becomes greater.

August 6
The Importance of Self-Reflection

Self-reflection is a vital part of the recovery journey. It's through honest reflection that awareness is developed, allowing for the identification of harmful patterns and the understanding of what needs to change.

Reflection requires honesty. It's not always easy to look at the areas of life where mistakes have been made or where growth is needed, but it's necessary for healing. Through reflection, there's a deeper understanding of self and the motivations that drive actions.

Self-reflection brings clarity. It offers insight into what's working, what's not, and where adjustments need to be made. With this clarity, the path forward in recovery becomes more defined, and the ability to make conscious choices is strengthened.

August 7
The Gift of Vulnerability

Vulnerability is often seen as a weakness, but in reality, it's a strength. In recovery, being vulnerable means being open, honest, and authentic, even when it's uncomfortable. Vulnerability is what allows for connection, healing, and growth.

Opening up can feel risky. The fear of judgment, rejection, or being misunderstood often prevents vulnerability. But in truth, vulnerability invites connection. It allows for others to see and support the true self, creating deeper, more meaningful relationships. Vulnerability is freeing. It releases the need to hide behind masks or walls, making space for healing. Through vulnerability, recovery is deepened, as there is less need for pretense and more room for authenticity.

August 8
Accepting Imperfection

Perfection is an illusion, and the pursuit of it often leads to frustration and self-judgment. In recovery, it's essential to accept imperfection—not as a flaw, but as part of the human experience. Healing doesn't require perfection, only progress.

Imperfection is what makes each person unique. By accepting the areas where mistakes are made or where growth is still needed, there's greater compassion for oneself. This acceptance creates space for healing without the added pressure of trying to be perfect.

In accepting imperfection, recovery becomes more sustainable. The focus shifts from trying to be flawless to being real and authentic. Through this lens, mistakes are seen as learning opportunities rather than failures, and growth happens more naturally.

August 9
Finding Strength in Compassion

Compassion is a source of strength in recovery. Whether it's compassion for oneself or others, this quality softens the harsh edges of life's challenges. Compassion invites understanding, kindness, and the ability to offer support without judgment.

Compassion starts within. By treating oneself with kindness during difficult moments, healing is supported. Self-compassion reduces the internal pressure to be perfect and replaces it with an attitude of care and understanding.

The more compassion is practiced, the stronger it becomes. It extends outward to others, creating a ripple effect of kindness and support. Through compassion, recovery is nurtured, and the world becomes a softer, more forgiving place.

August 10
The Courage to Change

Change takes courage. It's not easy to step into the unknown, leave behind old habits, or confront uncomfortable truths. But in recovery, change is essential for growth. It requires bravery to let go of what is familiar and step into a new way of being.

Courage isn't the absence of fear; it's the willingness to act despite it. Change often brings up fear of the unknown or of failure, but with courage, it's possible to move through that fear and embrace the transformation that recovery offers.

The courage to change is what makes healing possible. Each act of bravery, no matter how small, builds momentum for further growth. By facing the fear of change, the path forward becomes clearer, and the possibilities for a healthier, more fulfilled life expand.

August 11
Patience with the Process

Recovery is not something that happens overnight. It's a gradual process that requires patience, persistence, and time. Learning to be patient with oneself and with the journey is essential in maintaining balance and focus on long-term goals.

Impatience often arises when progress feels slow or when setbacks occur. Yet, in these moments, it's important to remember that real growth takes time. There are no shortcuts to healing. Each step, no matter how small, contributes to the larger picture of recovery.

Patience nurtures the process. It allows space for mistakes and learning, and it creates a sense of ease in the face of challenges. With patience, the mind can settle, and the journey of recovery can unfold in its natural time.

August 12
Embracing Uncertainty

Uncertainty is a part of life, and it can feel particularly unsettling during recovery. The unknowns—about the future, relationships, and even personal growth—can create anxiety. Learning to embrace uncertainty is a key to finding peace in recovery.

The mind often seeks certainty as a way to feel safe and in control. Yet, much of life is unpredictable. Embracing uncertainty means letting go of the need to know everything and instead finding comfort in the present moment.

Uncertainty brings possibilities. When there's openness to not knowing, new paths and opportunities can emerge. Recovery is about learning to live with this uncertainty, knowing that everything will unfold as it should, in its own time.

August 13
The Power of Small Steps

Recovery is often built on the foundation of small, consistent steps. While it's easy to focus on the big picture or long-term goals, it's the smaller actions taken each day that create lasting change.

Small steps may seem insignificant, but over time, they add up. Each moment of mindfulness, every healthy choice, and each instance of self-care contributes to the larger goal of healing. Recovery is a marathon, not a sprint, and it's the small steps that move the journey forward.

There's power in the present moment. By focusing on what can be done today, rather than worrying about the future or dwelling on the past, recovery becomes more manageable. Small steps, taken consistently, lead to significant progress over time.

August 14
The Art of Acceptance

Acceptance is one of the most powerful tools in recovery. It doesn't mean giving up or settling, but rather acknowledging what is, without resistance. By accepting the present moment as it is, peace and clarity can be found, even in difficult circumstances.

Resisting reality only creates more suffering. Whether it's a situation, a feeling, or a person, trying to control what cannot be changed leads to frustration and pain. Acceptance, on the other hand, allows space for healing and growth.

In accepting things as they are, there's freedom. Acceptance opens the door to finding solutions, making peace with the past, and embracing the present moment. It's the foundation of a balanced and grounded recovery process.

August 15
Listening to Inner Wisdom

Deep within, there is an inner wisdom that knows what is needed for healing. It's easy to get caught up in external advice, opinions, or the noise of the mind, but by quieting down and listening within, clarity can be found.

Inner wisdom often speaks softly, in moments of stillness and quiet. It's the intuition that knows what is right, even when the mind is confused or overwhelmed. Trusting this inner voice is key to navigating recovery with authenticity and truth.

By tuning into inner wisdom, guidance is found. It leads the way, offering insight into what is needed for growth and healing. Recovery is not about following a rigid path but rather about listening to what feels right in each moment.

August 16
Releasing Control

The desire to control outcomes, people, or situations often leads to stress and frustration. In recovery, learning to release control is essential for peace of mind and spiritual growth. Letting go of control doesn't mean giving up, but rather trusting that things will unfold as they are meant to.

Control is often rooted in fear—fear of the unknown, fear of failure, or fear of being hurt. Yet, the more tightly control is held, the more stressful life becomes. Letting go allows for a sense of ease, trust, and flow.

In releasing control, there's freedom. The burden of trying to manage everything lifts, and space is created for life to unfold naturally. Recovery becomes more peaceful when there's trust in the process rather than a constant need to control it.

August 17
The Healing Power of Forgiveness

Forgiveness is a powerful tool for healing, both in recovery and in life. Holding onto resentment or anger only harms the one holding it. Forgiveness, on the other hand, frees the heart and mind from the weight of past hurts.

Forgiving doesn't mean condoning harmful actions or forgetting what happened. It means letting go of the emotional charge and releasing the need for retribution. Forgiveness is an act of self-compassion, creating space for healing to take place.

When forgiveness is embraced, peace follows. It allows for freedom from the past and the ability to move forward with clarity and lightness. Recovery becomes easier when forgiveness is part of the journey, both for oneself and for others.

August 18
The Strength of Humility

Humility is often misunderstood as weakness, but in reality, it is a strength. In recovery, humility means being open to learning, acknowledging mistakes, and remaining teachable. It's the recognition that growth is a continuous process.

Humility creates space for wisdom. By acknowledging that there's always more to learn, a deeper understanding is developed. Humility allows for connection with others, as it removes the barriers of pride and opens the heart to compassion.

Humility strengthens recovery. It encourages honesty, vulnerability, and a willingness to change. In the absence of ego, growth happens more freely, and the journey toward healing becomes smoother.

August 19

The Value of Gratitude

Gratitude is a simple yet profound practice that can transform the recovery process. By focusing on what is good, even in challenging moments, gratitude shifts the perspective and brings more joy and contentment into life.

It's easy to focus on what's lacking or what's going wrong, but gratitude redirects attention to what is already present. By appreciating the small moments, the beauty of life becomes more visible, even in the midst of recovery struggles.

Gratitude nourishes the spirit. It fosters a sense of abundance and helps to cultivate a more positive outlook. Recovery is enriched by gratitude, as it brings lightness and ease to the journey.

August 20
The Balance of Effort and Ease

Recovery is a balance between effort and ease. Too much effort can lead to burnout, while too much ease can result in stagnation. Finding the balance between these two forces is key to maintaining momentum without overwhelming the mind or body.

Effort is necessary for growth. It's the energy that drives change and keeps the recovery process moving forward. But effort alone isn't sustainable without moments of rest, reflection, and ease.

When effort is balanced with ease, recovery becomes more harmonious. There's a flow to the process that allows for both action and rest, pushing forward without becoming overwhelmed. This balance creates a steady, sustainable path to healing.

August 21
Trusting the Journey

The recovery process is full of twists and turns, and it's not always clear what lies ahead. Trusting the journey, even when the path seems uncertain, is essential. There will be challenges, but these challenges provide opportunities for growth and transformation.

Trust doesn't mean having all the answers. It means believing in the process, knowing that even when things feel difficult, they are part of a larger picture. Recovery is a journey of self-discovery, one that unfolds in its own time.

When trust is cultivated, anxiety and fear lessen. The need to control outcomes fades, and there is space for acceptance. Trusting the journey brings peace, allowing for a deeper connection to the present moment and the path of recovery.

August 22
Letting Go of Perfection

Perfectionism can be a barrier to recovery. The constant pressure to do things perfectly can create unnecessary stress and hinder progress. Letting go of perfection and embracing imperfection as part of the human experience allows for more freedom and growth.

Perfection is an illusion. No one is perfect, and striving for perfection often leads to frustration and disappointment. Instead, it's important to focus on progress, not perfection. Small improvements, mistakes, and setbacks are all part of the journey.

In letting go of perfection, there's room for self-compassion. It becomes easier to accept oneself as they are, flaws and all, and to continue moving forward without the weight of unrealistic expectations.

August 23
The Importance of Rest

In the fast pace of life, it's easy to overlook the need for rest. Yet, rest is essential for both physical and emotional recovery. It's in moments of stillness that the mind and body can rejuvenate, heal, and regain strength.

Rest is not a sign of weakness or laziness. It's a necessary part of the recovery process. Pushing too hard without rest can lead to burnout, making it harder to stay on track. True recovery comes from balancing effort with rest.

By honoring the need for rest, space is created for reflection and renewal. Resting doesn't mean stopping; it means allowing time to recharge, so that the journey can continue with energy and clarity.

August 24
Finding Purpose in Service

Service to others is a core component of recovery. It shifts the focus from self to the needs of others and brings a sense of purpose and fulfillment. Serving others in recovery is not only a way to give back, but it also strengthens one's own journey.

Service creates connection. It fosters a sense of community and shared experience, reminding everyone that they are not alone on this path. Acts of kindness, support, and understanding build bonds that help sustain recovery.

In giving, there is receiving. Service enriches the spirit, bringing joy and a sense of meaning. Whether small or large, acts of service are a powerful tool for maintaining recovery and deepening personal growth.

August 25

The Power of Surrender

Surrender is often misunderstood as giving up, but in recovery, surrender is about letting go of resistance and allowing the process to unfold naturally. It's an act of trust—trust in the journey, trust in the self, and trust in the wisdom of the present moment.

Surrender means accepting what cannot be controlled. It's a recognition that not everything can be changed, and that's okay. By releasing the need to fight against reality, there's space for peace and clarity to emerge.

Surrender brings freedom. It removes the weight of constant striving and struggling, allowing for a more relaxed and open-hearted approach to recovery. Surrendering to the process opens the door to deeper healing.

August 26
Resilience in the Face of Challenges

Challenges are inevitable in recovery, but resilience is the ability to face them with courage and strength. It's the inner resource that keeps one moving forward, even when things are difficult.

Resilience doesn't mean avoiding challenges; it means learning to navigate them with grace and perseverance. Each challenge is an opportunity to grow stronger, to learn more about oneself, and to develop new coping skills.

Building resilience takes time. It comes from facing difficulties, learning from them, and continuing to move forward. Resilience is the foundation that supports long-term recovery, allowing for greater strength and endurance on the path.

August 27

The Gift of Compassion

Compassion, both for oneself and for others, is a cornerstone of recovery. It's the ability to offer kindness, understanding, and forgiveness, even in the face of mistakes or setbacks. Compassion softens the heart and opens the mind to healing.

Self-compassion is often the hardest to practice. It's easy to be critical or harsh with oneself, especially when recovery feels slow or difficult. Yet, offering compassion to oneself is essential for maintaining balance and inner peace.

Compassion for others fosters connection. It reminds us that everyone is on their own journey, facing their own challenges. By practicing compassion, the heart opens to love and understanding, creating a more supportive and empathetic recovery process.

August 28
The Value of Vulnerability

Vulnerability is often seen as a weakness, but in recovery, it's a strength. Being vulnerable means being open, honest, and authentic about feelings, struggles, and fears. It's in vulnerability that true connection and healing can take place.

Vulnerability allows for growth. It creates space for others to offer support and understanding, and it fosters deeper connections in relationships. When the walls of defense come down, the heart opens, allowing for greater healing.

In recovery, vulnerability is essential. It's through sharing struggles and being honest with oneself and others that growth occurs. Vulnerability leads to strength, as it opens the door to authentic living and true healing.

August 29
The Peace of Letting Go

Letting go is one of the most difficult yet liberating aspects of recovery. Whether it's letting go of old habits, toxic relationships, or unrealistic expectations, the process of letting go creates space for new possibilities and growth.

Letting go is not a one-time event but a continual practice. It's about releasing what no longer serves, even when it feels comfortable or familiar. The peace that follows letting go is a deep sense of freedom and openness to what is yet to come.

In letting go, the past no longer has power over the present. The future becomes less of a worry, and the present moment takes on more significance. Letting go brings peace, clarity, and a renewed sense of purpose in recovery.

August 30
Gratitude for the Present Moment

The present moment is all that truly exists, and in recovery, learning to appreciate the here and now is a valuable skill. Gratitude for the present moment brings a sense of peace and contentment, allowing for a more balanced and centered approach to recovery.

Often, the mind is preoccupied with the past or worried about the future, but gratitude shifts the focus back to the present. In the present moment, there is peace, healing, and the opportunity to make mindful choices.

Gratitude for the present strengthens recovery. It helps to reduce anxiety, fosters a sense of well-being, and reminds us that each moment is an opportunity for growth and healing. Living in the present brings deeper fulfillment and joy.

August 31
The Journey of Self-Discovery

Recovery is a journey of self-discovery. It's an ongoing process of learning more about oneself, exploring inner strengths, and uncovering deeper truths. Each day brings new insights, challenges, and opportunities for growth.

The path of self-discovery is not always easy. It requires courage, honesty, and a willingness to face uncomfortable truths. Yet, it's through this process that the most profound healing occurs.

As the journey of self-discovery unfolds, a deeper connection to self and to life is formed. Recovery becomes not just about overcoming addiction, but about becoming more fully alive, more present, and more connected to the true self.

SEPTEMBER

254

September 1
The Power of Action

Action is what transforms intentions into reality. Recovery is not just about thinking or feeling differently, but about making deliberate choices that support healing and growth. Action is where the rubber meets the road.

Often, there is a temptation to wait until everything feels perfect before acting. But recovery doesn't wait for perfection—it requires stepping forward, even when things feel uncertain. Taking action, no matter how small, creates momentum.

In the process of recovery, the actions taken shape the path ahead. Whether it's reaching out for help, setting boundaries, or practicing mindfulness, each action is a step toward deeper healing and transformation.

September 2
Consistency in Recovery

Consistency is key to progress in recovery. It's not about grand gestures or massive changes overnight, but about showing up, day after day, and making choices that align with the intention to heal.

Recovery is built on small, consistent actions—whether it's attending meetings, practicing meditation, or simply choosing not to engage in harmful behaviors. Each consistent step reinforces the commitment to the process.

Consistency brings stability. It creates a foundation that can be relied upon, even in moments of difficulty or doubt. Through consistent actions, recovery becomes not just something done occasionally but a way of life.

September 3
The Courage to Act

Taking action often requires courage, especially in the face of fear or uncertainty. The unknown can be intimidating, and the prospect of change can trigger discomfort. Yet, it is through courageous action that growth occurs.

Courage isn't the absence of fear—it's the willingness to act despite it. In recovery, courage means stepping into the unfamiliar, trusting that each step forward is part of the healing process.

By choosing courage over fear, new possibilities open up. The willingness to take risks, to face challenges, and to step outside of comfort zones creates space for deeper healing and transformation.

September 4
Taking Responsibility

Recovery calls for taking responsibility for one's own choices and actions. This doesn't mean carrying the weight of the past with guilt or shame, but it does mean acknowledging the role played in shaping the present.

Taking responsibility is empowering. It shifts the focus from blaming others or external circumstances to recognizing personal agency. With responsibility comes the ability to make different choices moving forward.

In taking responsibility, ownership of the recovery journey is embraced. The past cannot be changed, but the actions taken now will determine the future. Responsibility is the foundation of personal growth and transformation.

September 5
Small Steps, Big Change

Sometimes, the road to recovery can feel overwhelming. The distance between where things are and where they need to be seems vast. But the journey is made up of small, manageable steps, each one contributing to long-term change.

There's no need to tackle everything at once. Focusing on the next small step keeps things achievable and reduces the pressure of trying to do too much too soon. Each small victory builds upon the last, creating momentum.

In time, these small steps add up to significant change. Recovery is a marathon, not a sprint, and each day brings the opportunity to take one more step toward healing.

September 6
Embracing Mistakes as Lessons

Mistakes are inevitable on the recovery journey. But instead of seeing them as failures, they can be reframed as valuable lessons. Each misstep offers insight into what needs to be adjusted or refined moving forward.

Recovery is not about perfection. It's about learning, growing, and evolving. Mistakes provide the feedback needed to make better choices in the future. They are part of the process of becoming more aware and more resilient.

By embracing mistakes as opportunities for learning, the fear of failure diminishes. Mistakes become stepping stones on the path of recovery, guiding the way toward deeper understanding and growth.

September 7
Action and Intention

Action and intention go hand in hand. Intentions set the direction, but without action, they remain unfulfilled. Likewise, action without intention can become aimless or unproductive. When aligned, action and intention create powerful change.

Before taking action, it's helpful to pause and reflect on the underlying intention. Is the action supporting recovery, growth, and healing? When actions are rooted in positive intentions, they become more meaningful and effective.

Intention gives purpose to action. It ensures that each step taken is aligned with the broader goals of recovery and well-being. By acting with clear intention, the path forward becomes more focused and purposeful.

September 8
The Practice of Patience

Action requires patience. It's easy to become frustrated when results aren't immediate or when the progress seems slow. But recovery is a gradual process, and patience is key to sustaining it over the long term.

Patience allows for a more compassionate approach to recovery. It recognizes that change takes time and that healing is not linear. There will be ups and downs, but with patience, it becomes easier to stay committed to the process.

In cultivating patience, the pressure to rush or force progress eases. Instead, there is a sense of acceptance for where things are, knowing that with consistent effort, change will come in its own time.

September 9
Taking Action with Mindfulness

Mindfulness brings awareness to each action taken. It encourages moving through the day with intention, being fully present in each moment, and making conscious choices that support recovery.

When actions are taken mindfully, they become more deliberate and thoughtful. Whether it's a conversation, a task, or a decision, mindfulness ensures that actions are aligned with the goals of healing and growth.

Mindful action brings clarity. It prevents impulsive reactions or mindless behaviors that may undermine recovery. By acting with awareness, there is greater control over the direction of the recovery journey.

September 10
The Power of Commitment

Commitment is the engine that drives recovery forward. Without commitment, the best intentions and plans can falter. True commitment comes from within, fueled by the desire for change and the willingness to do what it takes to achieve it.

Commitment means showing up, even when it's difficult or inconvenient. It means prioritizing recovery over distractions or temptations. With commitment, the path of recovery becomes non-negotiable, something that is followed with consistency and resolve.

In the face of challenges, commitment provides the strength to keep going. It's a reminder of why the journey was started in the first place and a promise to oneself to stay the course, no matter what obstacles arise.

September 11
Turning Over Control

One of the challenges in recovery is learning to let go of control. There's often a deep-seated desire to manage or manipulate outcomes, believing that things will be better if they can just be controlled. But the truth is, control is often an illusion.

Learning to let go means accepting that not everything can be controlled, and that's okay. Recovery involves surrendering to the process, allowing things to unfold as they will, without forcing or resisting. This doesn't mean inaction, but rather acting with acceptance of the things that cannot be changed.

In surrendering control, there's a sense of freedom. Without the constant need to manage every detail, energy is freed up for growth, healing, and responding to the present moment with clarity and grace.

September 12

Letting Go of Outcomes

Recovery asks that one learns to let go of outcomes. It's natural to have expectations and desires for how things should turn out, but becoming too attached to specific outcomes can lead to frustration and disappointment.

Letting go of outcomes means staying focused on the process rather than the result. It means taking action with the best of intentions and then releasing attachment to how things play out. The future is uncertain, and holding on too tightly to a desired outcome can create unnecessary stress.

By releasing the need to control outcomes, there's more space for things to unfold naturally. This brings a sense of peace and acceptance, knowing that as long as the right actions are taken, the rest will take care of itself.

September 13

Action in the Present Moment

The present moment is the only place where action can occur. It's easy to get caught up in thoughts about the future—worrying about what might happen, or trying to plan for every eventuality. But the future is shaped by the actions taken right now.

Staying grounded in the present allows for more mindful and effective action. There's no need to be overwhelmed by the unknown. Focusing on what can be done today brings a sense of calm and clarity.

By taking things one day at a time, the weight of the future lifts. The present moment holds all the power needed to move forward, and by acting in the here and now, the path ahead becomes clearer.

September 14
Trusting the Process

Recovery is a process, one that unfolds over time. It can be difficult to trust the process, especially when progress feels slow or when obstacles arise. But trust is an essential part of the journey.

Trusting the process means having faith that the actions taken today will lead to positive change, even if the results aren't immediately visible. It means believing in the power of recovery, and that with consistent effort, healing will come.

In moments of doubt, it's helpful to remember that recovery is not a linear path. There will be ups and downs, but by trusting the process and staying committed, each step forward brings greater strength and resilience.

September 15
Building Momentum

Momentum is built through consistent action. At first, the steps in recovery may feel small or insignificant, but over time, they add up. With each positive action, momentum grows, making it easier to continue moving forward.

Building momentum requires staying the course, even when it feels challenging. Each time an action is taken that supports recovery, it reinforces the commitment to healing. The more consistently these actions are taken, the more momentum builds, carrying things forward.

Momentum is a powerful force in recovery. It transforms small, daily efforts into lasting change. By focusing on taking one step at a time, the cumulative effect becomes a steady, unstoppable drive toward growth and healing.

September 16
The Ripple Effect of Action

Every action taken in recovery creates a ripple effect. A single choice can influence not only the immediate present but also the future, shaping outcomes in ways that may not be immediately apparent.

Just as a pebble dropped into water creates ripples that spread outward, actions in recovery have far-reaching consequences. Choosing mindfulness, compassion, and self-care in daily life affects not only personal well-being but also relationships, work, and the broader community. Being mindful of the ripple effect reminds that even small actions have power. Each decision contributes to the overall trajectory of the recovery journey, influencing both the immediate experience and the path ahead.

September 17
Staying Aligned with Core Values

Taking action in recovery means staying aligned with core values. It's easy to lose sight of what matters most when caught up in the busyness of life or the challenges of recovery, but core values provide a compass that guides every step.

Reflecting on what truly matters—whether it's honesty, integrity, compassion, or self-respect—helps in making choices that are aligned with the higher self. Actions rooted in these values strengthen the foundation of recovery and create a sense of purpose.

When actions align with values, recovery becomes more than just a set of behaviors; it becomes a way of living authentically. This alignment brings a sense of fulfillment and clarity, supporting long-term growth and well-being.

September 18
Overcoming Resistance to Action

Resistance often arises when facing difficult actions in recovery. Whether it's fear, doubt, or the comfort of old habits, resistance can block progress. But resistance is not a sign of failure—it's a natural part of the recovery process.

The key to overcoming resistance is acknowledging its presence without letting it control the decision-making process. Resistance is often a signal that something important is at stake, and by facing it head-on, growth becomes possible.

By recognizing and moving through resistance, greater strength is built. Each time resistance is overcome, confidence in the ability to take action grows, making it easier to move forward with courage and resolve.

September 19
The Power of Forgiveness in Action

Forgiveness is a powerful action in recovery. It's not about condoning harmful behavior or ignoring the pain caused, but about releasing the grip of resentment, anger, or guilt that can hold back progress.

Forgiveness starts with oneself. Recognizing past mistakes and letting go of self-judgment opens the door to healing. This internal forgiveness creates space for change, allowing room for compassion and self-acceptance.

Extending forgiveness to others brings a sense of freedom. It doesn't erase the past, but it lightens the emotional burden, making room for peace. In recovery, forgiveness becomes an act of liberation, freeing the mind from the weight of old wounds.

September 20
Taking Ownership of the Journey

Recovery is deeply personal. It's a journey that no one else can take, and one that requires full ownership. This means recognizing that the path forward is shaped by personal choices, actions, and attitudes.

Taking ownership doesn't mean shouldering the blame for everything that has happened. Instead, it's about recognizing the power to shape the present and future through conscious decisions. Taking responsibility for the journey empowers greater control over the outcomes. Ownership also brings freedom. When the journey is fully embraced, there's no longer a need to rely on others to create change. The path becomes clearer, guided by personal agency and the inner strength cultivated through recovery.

September 21
Accepting What Is

Acceptance is a key principle in recovery. It's easy to wish for things to be different, to long for a past that no longer exists or a future that seems uncertain. But true growth comes from accepting things as they are, without judgment or resistance.

Acceptance doesn't mean resignation. It means acknowledging reality as it is, without trying to change or control it. From this place of acceptance, clearer decisions can be made, and the next steps forward can be taken with more peace of mind.

By accepting what is, the mind becomes less reactive and more balanced. The energy that was once used to resist the present can now be used to heal, to move forward, and to grow. Acceptance creates space for progress.

September 22
Releasing Old Patterns

Old patterns and habits can be hard to break, especially when they've been a way of coping for so long. In recovery, recognizing these patterns is the first step toward change. Often, these habits no longer serve the person who is working toward healing.

Releasing old patterns isn't about rejecting the past or being harsh on oneself. It's about noticing when old behaviors no longer align with the new path. It involves bringing awareness to the automatic reactions and asking, "Does this still serve me?"

Once these patterns are identified, new choices can be made. Letting go of what no longer fits opens the door to healthier, more constructive behaviors. Each day in recovery is an opportunity to break free from the chains of the past and embrace a new way of being.

September 23
The Practice of Patience

Patience is essential in recovery, but it's often one of the most difficult practices to cultivate. Progress can feel slow, and setbacks are inevitable. However, patience is the quiet strength that allows for continued growth, even when immediate results aren't visible.

Patience teaches that healing is a gradual process. It reminds that real, lasting change takes time and that each small step forward is meaningful. In moments of frustration, patience allows one to pause and trust in the long-term journey.

By practicing patience, there's a recognition that every effort counts, even if the destination isn't reached today. The path of recovery is walked one step at a time, and with patience, each step brings its own value and lessons.

September 24
The Power of Routine

A solid routine can be a powerful ally in recovery. Having a daily structure provides a sense of stability, creating a framework that supports healing and growth. A routine doesn't have to be rigid, but it helps to have consistent practices that keep things grounded.

Establishing routines around mindfulness, self-care, and healthy habits builds a foundation for success. Even simple rituals, such as a morning meditation or journaling practice, create touchstones that offer balance and clarity throughout the day.

When the mind becomes restless or uncertain, returning to these routines can offer comfort. A reliable routine reminds one of the commitment to recovery and helps create a sense of purpose, making each day feel more intentional and focused.

September 25
Embracing Simplicity

There is a beauty in simplicity. In a world that often feels chaotic and overwhelming, simplifying life can bring a deep sense of peace. Recovery provides an opportunity to let go of distractions and focus on what truly matters. Embracing simplicity means clearing away the unnecessary—whether it's physical clutter, emotional baggage, or mental distractions. By simplifying, space is created for clarity, presence, and meaningful connection. A simple life doesn't mean a lack of richness. In fact, by focusing on what's essential, there's more room for joy, peace, and fulfillment. Recovery invites the practice of living with intention, where less is often more, and simplicity leads to greater freedom.

September 26
Acknowledging Progress

In the midst of recovery, it's easy to overlook the progress that's been made. The focus can often be on how far there is to go, rather than how far one has come. But recognizing and celebrating progress is crucial for maintaining motivation and self-compassion.

Progress doesn't have to be dramatic to be significant. Every small victory—whether it's a shift in mindset, a healthier choice, or a moment of clarity—is a step forward. Recovery is built on these small, steady improvements.

Acknowledging progress fosters a sense of gratitude and reinforces the belief that change is possible. By looking back on how much has been achieved, there's a renewed sense of purpose to continue moving forward.

September 27
The Importance of Rest

Rest is an essential part of recovery. In a culture that often prioritizes productivity, it can be difficult to allow time for rest without feeling guilty. But true healing requires moments of rest and renewal.

Rest doesn't just mean physical sleep—it also means allowing the mind and spirit to relax. Taking time to pause, reflect, and recharge is just as important as taking action. Without rest, the body and mind can become overwhelmed, leading to burnout.

By honoring the need for rest, a deeper balance is created. Rest allows for integration of all the lessons and growth in recovery, creating space for healing to unfold naturally and fully.

September 28
Trusting Intuition

Intuition is a valuable guide in recovery. Often, the mind is filled with noise—thoughts, fears, doubts—that can cloud judgment. But beneath this noise is a quiet, inner knowing. Learning to trust this intuition can provide clarity and direction.

Intuition isn't about overthinking; it's about tuning into that deep, inner wisdom that often speaks quietly but clearly. It's the gut feeling that guides decisions, the subtle sense of what feels right.

By trusting intuition, there's a stronger connection to one's true self. It becomes easier to make choices that align with recovery and personal growth. Listening to this inner voice brings a sense of confidence and trust in the journey.

September 29
Practicing Gratitude

Gratitude is a transformative practice in recovery. When the mind is focused on what's lacking or what's gone wrong, it can be easy to fall into a negative mindset. But gratitude shifts the focus to what's present, what's working, and what's good.

Practicing gratitude doesn't mean ignoring challenges or pretending everything is perfect. It's about acknowledging the small blessings, even in difficult times. By cultivating gratitude, a sense of abundance grows, and the mind becomes more open to positivity.

Gratitude fosters resilience. It reminds that despite the hardships, there is always something to appreciate, no matter how small. This shift in perspective strengthens the spirit and supports the recovery process.

September 30
Walking the Path

Recovery is a path, not a destination. There will be moments of struggle, moments of triumph, and moments of stillness. What matters most is the commitment to stay on the path, no matter where it leads.

Walking the path of recovery means showing up each day with intention and openness. It means embracing the journey as it is, with all its challenges and rewards, knowing that each step forward is part of a larger process.

The path of recovery is one of growth, healing, and self-discovery. By walking it with mindfulness and purpose, the journey becomes a source of strength and transformation.

OCTOBER

October 1

Letting Go of Control

The desire to control outcomes can be strong, especially in recovery. There's a need to feel secure, to know exactly what will happen next, to steer life in a certain direction. But much of life is beyond control, and clinging too tightly only creates suffering.

Letting go of control doesn't mean giving up responsibility. Instead, it means recognizing what can be influenced and what cannot. It involves releasing the need for certainty and allowing life to unfold naturally, trusting in the process rather than forcing results.

In recovery, the practice of letting go opens up space for acceptance, ease, and growth. It invites trust in oneself and in the journey, making room for new possibilities to emerge without the strain of rigid expectations.

October 2
The Power of Surrender

Surrender is often misunderstood as weakness, but in recovery, it's a powerful act of strength. Surrender means releasing the struggle against reality and accepting things as they are. It's about recognizing that not everything can be controlled or fixed by sheer willpower. True surrender doesn't mean giving up; it means acknowledging the limits of control and allowing something greater to guide the way. It's a practice of humility, accepting that sometimes the best way forward is to release resistance.

In moments of surrender, a sense of peace arises. The weight of trying to manage everything lifts, creating room for grace and healing. Surrendering opens the heart to new ways of being, beyond the limitations of control.

October 3

Embracing Uncertainty

Uncertainty is a natural part of life, but it can feel unsettling, especially in recovery. The unknown brings with it fear and doubt, creating a sense of vulnerability. However, learning to embrace uncertainty is a vital part of the recovery process.

Instead of fearing the unknown, one can learn to accept it with curiosity. What possibilities lie ahead? What new opportunities might arise? When the need for certainty is released, there's room for growth and discovery.

Embracing uncertainty isn't about seeking answers—it's about being present with the questions. It's about finding comfort in the not-knowing and trusting that the path will reveal itself, step by step.

October 4
Finding Strength in Vulnerability

Vulnerability can often feel like a weakness, but it's actually a profound source of strength. In recovery, opening up to vulnerability is essential for healing. It means being honest with oneself and others, acknowledging fears, emotions, and imperfections.

Strength doesn't come from putting up walls or pretending to have it all together. True strength is found in the willingness to be seen as imperfect, to admit when help is needed, and to face difficult emotions with courage.

By embracing vulnerability, there's a deeper connection with the self and with others. It creates a space for authentic healing, where true strength is built from honesty and openness, rather than from a façade of control.

October 5
The Wisdom of Patience

Patience is often tested in recovery. The mind wants quick fixes, immediate results, and clear answers, but true healing takes time. Patience is the practice of trusting that everything unfolds at its own pace, even when progress seems slow.

Impatience stems from a desire to control the outcome, but patience teaches that the process is more important than the destination. Each moment of struggle, growth, and change is a step toward wholeness, even when it's not immediately visible.

With patience, a deeper wisdom is cultivated—the understanding that the journey is long, and each small step forward is meaningful. It brings peace to the present moment, releasing the need for everything to happen on a fixed timeline.

October 6
Building Trust in the Process

Recovery is a process, not a single event. There are ups and downs, setbacks and breakthroughs, and it can be difficult to trust that the process is working when progress feels slow. But trust is key—it's the belief that, with time and effort, healing is possible.

Trusting the process means letting go of the need for immediate results. It means recognizing that each step, no matter how small, is part of a larger journey. The path may not always be clear, but trust keeps one moving forward.

By trusting the process, there's a release of fear and doubt. It allows for the unfolding of recovery in its own time, without forcing or rushing. Trust creates a foundation of faith in oneself and in the journey, even when the road is challenging.

October 7
Facing Fear with Courage

Fear is a natural part of recovery. Fear of failure, fear of the unknown, fear of change—it all arises at different points along the path. But courage isn't the absence of fear; it's the decision to move forward despite it.

Facing fear doesn't mean trying to eliminate it. Instead, it involves acknowledging fear without letting it take control. Fear can be a teacher, pointing to areas where growth is needed, where healing is possible.

By facing fear with courage, the grip it holds loosens. The more it's confronted, the less power it has. Courage builds confidence, allowing for deeper healing and greater strength in the recovery process.

October 8
Nurturing Compassion

Compassion is the heart of recovery. It's easy to be harsh and critical of oneself, especially when mistakes are made or progress is slow. But compassion invites a gentler approach, one that allows for mistakes and embraces imperfection.

Self-compassion is the practice of treating oneself with the same kindness that would be offered to a loved one. It means recognizing that recovery is hard, that setbacks happen, and that healing takes time.

By nurturing compassion, a safe space is created for growth. Compassion doesn't mean avoiding responsibility—it means acknowledging that mistakes are part of the process and that healing requires patience, understanding, and care.

October 9
The Gift of Mindfulness

Mindfulness is a powerful tool in recovery. It's the practice of bringing full awareness to the present moment, without judgment or distraction. In a world filled with noise and busyness, mindfulness creates a space for clarity and peace.

Through mindfulness, the mind becomes more focused, and reactions become less automatic. It helps in noticing thoughts, emotions, and behaviors without getting caught up in them. This awareness is key to breaking old patterns and cultivating healthier choices.

By practicing mindfulness, the present moment becomes a place of refuge. It provides an anchor in recovery, offering a calm center amidst the storms of life. The gift of mindfulness is the ability to see clearly, to respond thoughtfully, and to live more fully.

October 10
Releasing Guilt and Shame

Guilt and shame can weigh heavily in recovery. They are powerful emotions that can keep one stuck in the past, reliving mistakes and feeling unworthy of healing. But holding onto guilt and shame only prolongs suffering.

Releasing guilt and shame doesn't mean ignoring past actions or avoiding responsibility. It means acknowledging mistakes, making amends where possible, and choosing to forgive oneself. Recovery is about learning from the past, not being defined by it.

By letting go of guilt and shame, there's freedom to move forward with self-compassion and clarity. The past doesn't have to dictate the future. In recovery, there's always the opportunity to begin again, to learn, to grow, and to heal.

October 11
The Practice of Acceptance

Acceptance is one of the hardest yet most rewarding practices in recovery. It doesn't mean liking or condoning everything that happens but rather recognizing reality as it is without resistance. By accepting what cannot be changed, the focus shifts to what can be done here and now.

Fighting against reality only increases suffering. When something doesn't go as planned, it's easy to resist, to wish it were different. But this resistance only deepens pain. Acceptance, on the other hand, offers peace. It allows for the present moment to be experienced fully, without the weight of resistance.

In recovery, acceptance is the foundation of growth. By accepting things as they are—flaws, mistakes, setbacks—there is room to learn and to heal. Acceptance doesn't mean passivity; it's the starting point for real and lasting change.

October 12
The Power of Gratitude

Gratitude transforms the way life is experienced. Even in moments of difficulty, there is always something to be grateful for, and this perspective brings a sense of peace and contentment. Gratitude shifts focus away from lack and toward abundance, from what's wrong to what's right.

In recovery, practicing gratitude helps build resilience. It's easy to focus on what has been lost, the struggles faced, and the challenges ahead. But gratitude reminds that, despite all of this, there is still so much to be thankful for—growth, support, even the simple breath in this moment.

Gratitude is more than just a feeling; it's a practice. By intentionally seeking out things to be grateful for each day, the heart opens, and the mind becomes more focused on positivity and hope. It changes not only how recovery is viewed but how life is experienced.

October 13
Embracing Humility

Humility is a quiet strength that supports recovery. It's the recognition that no one has all the answers and that everyone is constantly learning and growing. Humility is not about lowering oneself but about understanding the true nature of the self—imperfect, yet capable of growth. In recovery, humility is essential. It helps in letting go of ego and pride, allowing for a willingness to seek help, admit mistakes, and learn from others. Humility softens the need to be right and makes space for honest reflection and openness to change.

Embracing humility allows for deeper connection with oneself and with others. It fosters compassion, patience, and understanding, making the recovery journey more authentic and grounded in real strength—the strength of vulnerability and openness.

October 14
Cultivating Inner Peace

Inner peace is not something that can be found outside—it's cultivated from within. The world is full of chaos and uncertainty, but peace can always be found in the stillness of the heart. Cultivating this peace requires practice, patience, and a commitment to living mindfully. In recovery, finding inner peace may feel elusive at times, especially when emotions are intense and challenges arise. But by turning inward and practicing mindfulness, meditation, and self-compassion, a deep sense of calm can be nurtured. This peace is not about escaping reality but about facing it with clarity and calmness.

When inner peace is cultivated, it becomes easier to respond to life's challenges with grace and resilience. It offers a refuge from the storms of life and creates a strong foundation for healing and growth in recovery.

October 15

Learning to Forgive

Forgiveness is a vital step in the recovery journey. It's not about excusing harmful actions but about releasing the emotional burden that comes with holding onto resentment and anger. Forgiveness is an act of liberation, freeing both oneself and others from the grip of past pain. In recovery, forgiving oneself is often the hardest part. The mind holds onto mistakes, replaying them over and over, creating guilt and shame. But without self-forgiveness, it's impossible to move forward. Forgiving doesn't mean forgetting—it means acknowledging the hurt and choosing to let go for the sake of healing.

True forgiveness opens the heart and creates space for compassion, both for oneself and for others. It allows the healing process to deepen, releasing the emotional chains that keep the past alive in the present.

October 16
Patience with the Process

Recovery is a journey, not a destination. It's easy to become impatient when progress feels slow, but patience is key to long-term success. Healing takes time, and there will be setbacks along the way. Patience allows space for mistakes and growth without rushing the process.

In moments of frustration, remember that each step forward, no matter how small, is meaningful. Progress isn't always visible in the short term, but over time, the cumulative effect of patience and persistence leads to lasting change.

Patience also cultivates a sense of peace in the present moment. It allows for acceptance of where things are now, without the pressure to achieve immediate results. With patience, the journey becomes more manageable, and healing unfolds naturally.

October 17
Acknowledging Progress

In recovery, it's easy to focus on what still needs to be done, overlooking the progress that has already been made. Acknowledging progress is essential for maintaining motivation and building self-confidence. Each step forward, no matter how small, is a victory worth celebrating.

Recovery is not about perfection—it's about progress. There will be setbacks, but those do not erase the growth that has already occurred. Taking time to recognize and celebrate even the smallest achievements builds resilience and encourages continued effort.

By acknowledging progress, there's a shift from a mindset of lack to one of abundance. It brings a sense of accomplishment and fosters hope for the future, reminding that each day of effort brings one closer to a healthier, more fulfilling life.

October 18
The Importance of Self-Compassion

Self-compassion is often overlooked in recovery, yet it's one of the most important tools for healing. It involves treating oneself with the same kindness and understanding that would be offered to a close friend. In moments of struggle, self-compassion creates a safe space for growth and reflection.

Recovery is hard, and there will be times of difficulty and failure. Without self-compassion, the tendency is to become self-critical, which only adds to the burden. But when self-compassion is practiced, it creates a sense of support and encouragement, allowing for a healthier, more sustainable recovery process.

With self-compassion, the journey becomes one of learning rather than punishment. Mistakes are seen as opportunities for growth, not reasons for self-judgment. This kindness toward oneself fosters resilience, making it easier to navigate the challenges of recovery.

October 19
Finding Balance

Balance is essential for maintaining long-term recovery. Life is full of competing demands, and it can be easy to become overwhelmed by one aspect while neglecting others. Finding balance means creating a harmonious way of living that supports both mental and physical well-being.

Recovery requires attention to many areas of life—physical health, emotional well-being, relationships, and spirituality. Balance ensures that no single area is neglected. It means making time for rest, self-care, and connection with others, all while continuing the work of healing.

Achieving balance is an ongoing process. It requires regular reflection and adjustment. By maintaining a balanced approach, recovery becomes more sustainable, allowing for a healthier, more fulfilling life.

October 20
Living with Intention

Living with intention means making conscious choices rather than reacting automatically to life's events. It involves setting clear priorities and aligning actions with values. In recovery, living with intention creates a sense of purpose and direction, making each day a meaningful step toward healing.

When life is lived without intention, it becomes easy to fall back into old habits and patterns. But with intention, each action is deliberate, chosen for its alignment with long-term recovery goals. This creates a sense of empowerment and control over one's life.

Living with intention also brings clarity and focus. It allows for thoughtful decision-making and helps in staying committed to the recovery path, even when challenges arise. With intention, life becomes a conscious, purposeful journey toward healing and growth.

October 21
Trusting the Journey

Trust is a vital element in recovery. Trusting the process, even when it feels uncertain, is what allows healing to unfold naturally. The path may not always be clear, but by trusting the journey, a sense of peace and confidence begins to grow.

Doubt and fear often creep in when progress feels slow or obstacles arise. It's easy to question whether things will ever improve. But trusting the journey means embracing the uncertainty and knowing that each step, no matter how small, is moving in the right direction.

With trust, it becomes easier to let go of control and flow with life's changes. This doesn't mean being passive; it means staying open and receptive, knowing that with perseverance, healing is inevitable.

October 22

Resilience in the Face of Adversity

Resilience is the ability to keep moving forward despite difficulties. It's the inner strength that allows for recovery, even when the path becomes rocky. Resilience is not about avoiding challenges but about responding to them with courage and determination.

In recovery, setbacks are inevitable. The real measure of growth is how those setbacks are handled. Instead of giving up when things get hard, resilience keeps the heart open, the mind focused, and the spirit strong. It's a reminder that difficulties are part of the journey, not the end of it.

Resilience builds with practice. Each time a challenge is met with strength, it becomes easier to face the next one. This process of rising after every fall creates a solid foundation for long-term recovery and growth.

October 23
Letting Go of Expectations

Expectations can be a source of suffering, especially when they go unmet. Recovery is about learning to let go of rigid expectations and embracing life as it unfolds. When expectations are released, there is more room for acceptance, gratitude, and peace.

It's natural to have hopes and goals in recovery, but clinging too tightly to specific outcomes creates disappointment. Life rarely unfolds exactly as planned, and recovery is no exception. Letting go of expectations allows for flexibility, adaptability, and the ability to flow with life's changes.

By releasing expectations, the focus shifts from outcomes to the present moment. It creates space for contentment and allows the recovery process to unfold organically, without the pressure of rigid demands.

October 24
Embracing Vulnerability

Vulnerability is often seen as a weakness, but in recovery, it's one of the greatest strengths. Being vulnerable means being open, honest, and authentic, even when it feels uncomfortable. It's through vulnerability that true connection, growth, and healing happen.

Hiding behind walls of protection may feel safe, but it isolates and hinders progress. Recovery requires breaking down those walls and allowing others to see the true self, flaws and all. Vulnerability is not about oversharing; it's about being real, both with oneself and with others.

Embracing vulnerability fosters deep connection, not only with others but with one's own heart. It allows for compassion, understanding, and the freedom to be imperfect, which is the essence of real, lasting recovery.

October 25
The Gift of Surrender

Surrender is often misunderstood. It's not about giving up but about letting go of the need for control. In recovery, surrender is the act of acknowledging that some things cannot be managed alone. It's about trusting a greater process and allowing help to come in.

The ego resists surrender, wanting to maintain control over everything. But in recovery, true healing begins when control is relinquished, and surrender becomes a conscious choice. Surrender is the doorway to freedom—it's the moment when help is accepted, and the path forward becomes clearer.

Surrender doesn't mean passivity; it means actively choosing to let go of what is no longer serving and trusting the journey ahead. In that space, healing becomes possible, and recovery takes on new depth and meaning.

October 26
Moving Beyond Fear

Fear is a natural emotion, but it can become a barrier to recovery if left unchecked. Moving beyond fear doesn't mean erasing it, but learning to face it with courage. Fear has a way of paralyzing growth, keeping the mind stuck in old patterns of avoidance and hesitation.

In recovery, fear often arises when stepping into the unknown, when old habits are challenged, or when change feels overwhelming. But by acknowledging fear and choosing to move through it, the mind becomes stronger, and the spirit more resilient.

Fear loses its power when it's faced with courage and clarity. It's not the absence of fear that signifies growth, but the ability to move forward despite it. Each step beyond fear is a step toward greater freedom and healing.

October 27
The Strength of Compassion

Compassion is not just a feeling—it's an active practice of kindness and understanding toward oneself and others. In recovery, compassion provides the strength to heal from past wounds and the patience to navigate present challenges. It softens the harsh edges of judgment and opens the heart to growth.

Practicing compassion begins with oneself. Often, the hardest person to show compassion to is the self. But without self-compassion, the recovery journey becomes harsh and unforgiving. Compassion allows for mistakes, acknowledges pain, and offers a path toward healing without judgment.

By cultivating compassion, both for oneself and for others, the journey of recovery becomes gentler and more sustainable. It fosters connection, healing, and the recognition that everyone is doing their best with the tools they have at the moment.

October 28
The Freedom of Forgiveness

Forgiveness is not a single act but a continual practice of releasing past hurt and choosing peace in the present moment. In recovery, forgiveness offers freedom from the emotional burdens of resentment and anger. It's not about excusing harm, but about letting go of the hold it has over the heart.

Forgiveness can be difficult, especially when wounds run deep. But by holding onto anger, suffering is prolonged. Forgiveness is an act of self-liberation. It's the recognition that by letting go of the past, healing becomes possible, and peace returns to the heart.

Forgiving oneself is equally important. Mistakes made in the past are part of the journey, but they do not define the future. By embracing forgiveness, the path ahead becomes clearer, and the heart lighter.

October 29
The Practice of Mindfulness

Mindfulness is the practice of being fully present in each moment, without judgment or distraction. In recovery, mindfulness creates the space to observe thoughts, feelings, and actions without becoming overwhelmed by them. It allows for a deeper understanding of the self and the present moment.

Mindfulness is not about escaping reality, but about fully engaging with it. It's about noticing what is happening, both internally and externally, with clarity and acceptance. Through mindfulness, the ups and downs of recovery are met with greater ease and understanding.

By cultivating mindfulness, it becomes possible to respond to life's challenges with calmness and presence, rather than reacting out of habit. This practice fosters emotional stability, mental clarity, and a deeper connection to the recovery process.

October 30
Honoring Progress

Progress in recovery is not always linear. There are moments of great growth and times when it feels like nothing is changing. But each small step forward, each moment of clarity, is worth honoring. Progress is not measured in perfection, but in the steady movement toward healing.

In moments of doubt, it's easy to forget how far things have come. Recovery is a journey, and progress is often gradual. By taking time to reflect on the progress that has been made, the heart fills with gratitude, and the mind becomes more focused on the path ahead.

Honoring progress is not about celebrating perfection, but about acknowledging effort, persistence, and growth. It's a reminder that, even in the smallest ways, each day brings the opportunity for healing and transformation.

October 31
Living with Gratitude

Gratitude is more than just an emotion—it's a way of living. In recovery, gratitude is the foundation for maintaining a positive and hopeful outlook. By focusing on what is good, rather than what is lacking, life becomes more joyful, and the recovery journey more fulfilling.

It's easy to overlook the many blessings in life, especially in times of struggle. But by practicing gratitude, even in small ways, the mind begins to shift from scarcity to abundance. Gratitude opens the heart and invites more peace and joy into the daily experience.

Living with gratitude is not about ignoring challenges, but about recognizing that, despite difficulties, there is always something to be thankful for. It's this practice that sustains hope and fosters deep healing in recovery.

NOVEMBER

November 1
The Power of Acceptance

Acceptance is one of the most profound tools in recovery. It doesn't mean resigning to circumstances but rather recognizing things as they are without the need to control or resist. In recovery, acceptance allows space for healing and growth by embracing the present moment.

Often, there's a tendency to fight against reality, to wish things were different or to dwell on the past. But fighting reality only causes more suffering. Acceptance, on the other hand, brings peace by allowing things to be as they are. It's the first step toward making meaningful change.

With acceptance comes the freedom to let go of unrealistic expectations and the need to control outcomes. Instead, there's an opportunity to focus on what can be changed and how to respond with grace and clarity. This is where true recovery begins to unfold.

November 2
Embracing Humility

Humility is about recognizing that no one has all the answers. It's the awareness that each person is a work in progress, always learning and evolving. Humility in recovery means acknowledging the need for help, whether from others or from a higher power.

Pride often gets in the way of asking for support. The ego wants to maintain an image of strength and independence, but real growth happens when the ego steps aside, allowing vulnerability and humility to take its place. This opens the door to true transformation.

By embracing humility, there's an openness to learning from every experience, every mistake, and every person encountered. It fosters a deep sense of connection, not only with others but also with the journey itself, leading to more authentic and sustainable recovery.

November 3
Learning from Mistakes

Mistakes are an inevitable part of life and recovery. Rather than viewing them as failures, mistakes can be seen as opportunities for learning and growth. Recovery is not about avoiding mistakes altogether, but about how one responds to them when they happen.

There can be a tendency to judge harshly when things don't go as planned. But this self-criticism only deepens the pain. Instead, learning to approach mistakes with curiosity and compassion allows for deeper understanding. Each misstep is a teacher, offering valuable lessons for the future.

By shifting the perspective on mistakes, they become stepping stones toward progress rather than barriers to success. The recovery journey is not defined by the absence of mistakes, but by the ability to learn from them and continue moving forward.

November 4
The Practice of Patience

Patience is essential in recovery. Healing takes time, and the road to recovery is often filled with challenges that require enduring effort. Patience allows for the slow unfolding of growth without rushing the process or becoming frustrated when things don't move as quickly as expected.

In moments of impatience, it's easy to become discouraged. But by practicing patience, a deeper appreciation for the small victories and subtle changes begins to emerge. Recovery is not a race but a journey that requires gentle persistence.

Patience is also about being kind to oneself, recognizing that change takes time. The ability to wait without becoming frustrated is a powerful practice that deepens resilience and allows healing to take root naturally.

November 5
Gratitude for the Present

Gratitude has the power to transform the recovery process by shifting the focus from what is lacking to what is present. Often, attention is directed toward problems, shortcomings, or what needs to be fixed. But by practicing gratitude, the present moment becomes enough.

Recovery offers countless moments to practice gratitude, whether for small steps forward or the support of others. Focusing on what is going well, even in challenging times, cultivates a sense of peace and contentment that helps sustain the journey.

Gratitude doesn't ignore the difficulties but places them in a wider perspective. It allows for the recognition that, despite the struggles, there is much to be thankful for, even in the process of healing itself.

November 6
Staying Grounded

Staying grounded in recovery means maintaining a sense of stability and presence, even in the midst of challenges. Life's ups and downs can create emotional turbulence, but staying grounded ensures that there's a steady foundation from which to navigate these fluctuations.

When feeling ungrounded, it's easy to become reactive or overwhelmed. Grounding practices, such as mindfulness or deep breathing, can help bring attention back to the present moment. These tools provide a refuge from the chaos and allow for a clearer perspective. Grounding isn't about ignoring emotions but finding a calm center from which to process them. By staying grounded, it becomes possible to respond to life with clarity and purpose rather than being swept away by its challenges.

November 7
Embracing Change

Change is a constant in life and in recovery. Whether it's the shift in mindset, behavior, or environment, change is an inevitable part of the process. Learning to embrace change rather than fear it creates a smoother path toward healing.

Resistance to change often stems from the desire for comfort and predictability. But clinging to the old ways can hinder progress. By seeing change as an opportunity for growth rather than a threat, the recovery process becomes more fluid and adaptive.

Embracing change doesn't mean rushing into it but staying open and curious about what it might bring. With openness to change, there's more room for transformation, allowing recovery to unfold in unexpected and beautiful ways.

November 8

Practicing Forgiveness

Forgiveness is a vital part of healing, both for oneself and others. Holding onto resentment or self-blame creates emotional barriers that hinder recovery. Forgiveness is not about condoning past actions but about releasing their hold on the heart.

Forgiving others for their mistakes, and oneself for missteps, allows for emotional freedom. It frees the mind from the burden of anger or guilt and opens the door to peace. The practice of forgiveness is a gift to oneself, creating space for deeper healing.

True forgiveness takes time and may require revisiting old wounds. But with each step toward forgiveness, the heart becomes lighter, and recovery becomes a more compassionate and self-affirming process.

November 9
Finding Balance

Balance is key in recovery. It's about finding a middle way between extremes, whether in thoughts, emotions, or actions. Too much focus on one area, at the expense of others, can lead to burnout or neglect. Balance creates harmony and sustainability in the recovery process.

There's often a temptation to throw all energy into one aspect of recovery, such as work or relationships, while neglecting others. But true recovery requires attention to all areas of life—physical, emotional, mental, and spiritual. Balance ensures that no part of life is left behind.

Achieving balance is not about perfection, but about making small adjustments to maintain equilibrium. By regularly checking in with oneself and making necessary shifts, balance becomes a guiding principle for long-term recovery and well-being.

November 10
Staying Present

The mind often drifts into the past or the future, creating anxiety or regret. Staying present is a core principle in recovery, allowing for a clear and focused mind. The present moment is where healing occurs, where decisions are made, and where growth happens.

It's easy to get caught up in worrying about what might happen or dwelling on past mistakes. But by anchoring attention in the present, recovery becomes more manageable. Each moment is an opportunity to choose wisely, to respond thoughtfully, and to take steps forward.

Staying present requires practice, but with time, it becomes second nature. The ability to focus on the here and now brings clarity, reduces stress, and fosters a deep sense of peace that sustains the recovery journey.

November 11
The Role of Compassion

Compassion is a cornerstone of healing and recovery. It involves extending kindness and understanding to oneself and others, recognizing that everyone is on their own journey and facing their own struggles. Compassion softens the harshness of self-judgment and encourages a more empathetic view of others.

In recovery, self-compassion is crucial. It's easy to be self-critical and harsh, especially when facing setbacks. Yet, compassion invites a more gentle and understanding approach, allowing for mistakes to be seen as part of the process rather than failures.

Cultivating compassion towards oneself and others fosters a supportive environment where healing can flourish. It transforms the recovery experience from one of isolation and struggle into a journey shared with empathy and care.

November 12
The Strength in Vulnerability

Vulnerability is often perceived as a weakness, but in reality, it is a profound strength. It involves opening up and being honest about one's struggles, fears, and hopes. In recovery, embracing vulnerability allows for deeper connections and more meaningful support.

Being vulnerable means letting go of the façade of perfection and admitting that help is needed. It's through this openness that genuine connections with others are formed, and true healing begins. Vulnerability creates space for authenticity and encourages others to share their own experiences.

Understanding that vulnerability is a strength rather than a weakness allows for a more genuine recovery experience. It fosters deeper relationships, more meaningful support, and a stronger sense of community.

November 13
Trusting the Process

Trusting the recovery process means having faith that, even if progress seems slow or uncertain, each step is moving toward healing. Trust involves letting go of the need to control every aspect of the journey and believing that things will unfold as they should.

Doubt and impatience can often cloud the recovery journey. However, trusting in the process allows for acceptance of the natural flow of growth and healing. It's about believing that every challenge and every small victory contributes to the overall journey.

Trusting the process encourages patience and persistence, knowing that each day brings progress, even if it is not immediately visible. This trust is a vital part of sustaining motivation and commitment throughout the recovery journey.

November 14
Nurturing Inner Strength

Inner strength is the quiet resolve that supports recovery through challenges and changes. It involves recognizing and drawing upon personal resilience and the ability to persevere, even in difficult times. Nurturing this strength helps sustain the journey and overcome obstacles.

Sometimes, it may feel like strength is running thin, but it is always present within. By acknowledging past successes and the ability to overcome previous challenges, inner strength can be reinforced and relied upon. This internal resource provides the courage needed to face ongoing challenges.

Nurturing inner strength involves self-reflection and acknowledging personal growth. It means recognizing the capacity to handle adversity and using that realization to move forward with confidence and determination.

November 15
The Journey of Self-Discovery

Recovery is not just about overcoming addiction but also about discovering who one truly is. This journey of self-discovery involves exploring personal values, passions, and aspirations, and understanding how they shape the recovery process.

Through recovery, a deeper understanding of oneself emerges. This includes recognizing strengths, areas for growth, and the ways in which one can contribute positively to life. Self-discovery enriches the recovery journey by aligning actions with personal truths and values.

Embracing self-discovery leads to a more authentic life. It transforms recovery from a mere process of change into a profound exploration of self, paving the way for a more fulfilling and purpose-driven life.

November 16
Celebrating Small Victories

Celebrating small victories is essential for maintaining motivation and acknowledging progress in recovery. Each small step forward, no matter how minor it may seem, contributes to the overall journey and deserves recognition.

Small victories provide evidence of progress and build confidence. They remind one that change is happening, even if the process feels slow. Celebrating these moments fosters a sense of accomplishment and reinforces the commitment to recovery.

Recognizing and celebrating small victories transforms the recovery journey into a series of achievable goals, creating a positive feedback loop that sustains motivation and reinforces the belief in continued growth.

November 17
Finding Joy in the Journey

Finding joy in the journey of recovery is about appreciating the moments of happiness and contentment that arise along the way. It involves recognizing and celebrating the positive aspects of life, even amidst the challenges.

Joy can be found in simple pleasures and in moments of connection and achievement. By focusing on these sources of joy, the recovery process becomes more enjoyable and fulfilling. It shifts the focus from what is lacking to what is already present and positive.

Embracing joy in recovery helps to balance the challenges with moments of happiness. It creates a more holistic view of the journey, where both struggles and joys coexist, making the process more enriching and balanced.

November 18
The Importance of Reflection

Reflection plays a crucial role in the recovery process. It involves looking back on experiences, understanding their significance, and applying the insights gained to future actions. Reflection provides a deeper understanding of oneself and the journey.

By regularly reflecting on experiences, one gains clarity and perspective. This practice helps to identify patterns, recognize growth, and understand the underlying causes of challenges. Reflection turns experiences into valuable lessons for continued growth and improvement.

Incorporating reflection into the recovery process enhances self-awareness and supports ongoing development. It transforms past experiences into tools for learning and growth, enriching the journey toward healing.

November 19
Embracing New Beginnings

Recovery is a continuous journey of new beginnings. Each day presents an opportunity to start fresh, to let go of past mistakes, and to embrace new possibilities. Embracing new beginnings involves approaching each day with a renewed sense of hope and possibility.

Letting go of the past and focusing on the present allows for a more open and optimistic outlook. Each new beginning is a chance to apply lessons learned, make positive changes, and move forward with a clear and determined mindset.

Embracing new beginnings fosters a sense of renewal and growth. It provides the motivation to continue the journey with enthusiasm and an open heart, seeing each day as a fresh start and a new opportunity for progress.

November 20
Cultivating Resilience

Resilience is the ability to bounce back from adversity and continue moving forward despite challenges. Cultivating resilience involves developing inner strength and coping strategies that support recovery and personal growth.

Resilience is built through experience, learning from setbacks, and adapting to change. It's about finding ways to overcome obstacles and maintain hope and determination. By focusing on resilience, one can navigate the ups and downs of recovery with greater ease.

Cultivating resilience strengthens the ability to face future challenges with confidence. It turns difficulties into opportunities for growth, reinforcing the commitment to recovery and personal development.

November 21
The Value of Support Networks

Support networks play a vital role in recovery, providing encouragement, guidance, and companionship. Building and maintaining strong connections with others fosters a sense of community and helps to navigate the recovery journey more effectively.

Support networks offer diverse perspectives, shared experiences, and practical assistance. They provide a safety net during challenging times and celebrate successes along the way. Engaging with supportive individuals enhances motivation and provides a sense of belonging.

The value of support networks lies in their ability to offer both practical help and emotional comfort. By nurturing these connections, the recovery journey becomes more collaborative and less solitary, enriching the experience and supporting sustained progress.

November 22
Letting Go of Perfectionism

Perfectionism often creates unrealistic expectations and self-imposed pressure. In recovery, letting go of perfectionism involves embracing imperfections and accepting that mistakes are a natural part of the journey. Striving for perfection can lead to frustration and discouragement. Instead, recognizing that progress is more important than perfection allows for a more compassionate and realistic approach to recovery. It's about valuing effort and growth rather than unattainable ideals.

Letting go of perfectionism creates space for genuine progress and self-acceptance. It fosters a more forgiving and encouraging environment, where the focus is on continuous improvement rather than impossible standards.

November 23
The Role of Self-Care

Self-care is an essential component of recovery, involving practices that nurture physical, emotional, and mental well-being. Prioritizing self-care helps to maintain balance and provides the necessary support for continued healing and growth.

Self-care includes activities that promote relaxation, health, and happiness. It involves setting aside time for oneself, engaging in activities that bring joy, and addressing personal needs. By prioritizing self-care, one can enhance overall well-being and sustain the recovery process.

The role of self-care in recovery is to provide a foundation of well-being from which to address challenges and pursue goals. It reinforces the importance of taking care of oneself as an integral part of the healing journey.

November 24
Embracing Patience with Self

Patience with oneself is about recognizing that healing is a gradual process that requires time and effort. Embracing patience involves being gentle and understanding with oneself, even when progress seems slow or difficult.

It's easy to become frustrated with oneself when facing setbacks or slow progress. However, practicing patience allows for a more compassionate and supportive approach to recovery. It's about accepting that each step, no matter how small, is part of the journey.

Embracing patience with oneself fosters a sense of self-compassion and resilience. It helps to maintain a positive outlook and encourages perseverance, making the recovery process more manageable and sustainable.

November 25
Finding Meaning in Challenges

Challenges are an inherent part of recovery, but they also offer opportunities for growth and insight. Finding meaning in challenges involves looking beyond the difficulties to discover the lessons and strengths they bring.

Challenges can provide valuable insights into personal resilience and the capacity to overcome adversity. By finding meaning in these experiences, one can gain a deeper understanding of oneself and the recovery process. It's about transforming obstacles into opportunities for growth.

Finding meaning in challenges enriches the recovery journey by providing perspective and motivation. It shifts the focus from the difficulties themselves to the growth and learning that arise from overcoming them.

November 26
The Joy of Giving

Giving to others can be a source of immense joy and fulfillment. In recovery, sharing one's experiences, time, or resources with others creates a sense of connection and purpose. The act of giving fosters a supportive and positive environment.

Giving doesn't have to be grand or dramatic; even small acts of kindness can have a significant impact. By contributing to the well-being of others, one also nurtures their own sense of purpose and belonging. Giving creates a cycle of positivity that benefits both the giver and the receiver.

The joy of giving enriches the recovery journey by fostering a sense of community and connection. It transforms recovery from an individual endeavor into a shared experience of support and generosity.

November 27
Celebrating Progress

Celebrating progress, no matter how incremental, is crucial in maintaining motivation and acknowledging achievements. Each step forward, however small, contributes to the overall journey of recovery and deserves recognition.

Recognizing progress helps to build confidence and reinforces the commitment to recovery. It's about appreciating the effort and growth that has occurred, rather than focusing solely on the end goal. Celebrations of progress create a positive and encouraging environment.

Celebrating progress fosters a sense of accomplishment and reinforces the belief in continued growth. It turns the recovery journey into a series of milestones, each one marking a step toward greater well-being.

November 28
The Value of Routine

Routine provides structure and stability in recovery, offering a sense of order and predictability. Establishing and maintaining a routine helps to create a balanced and manageable approach to daily life and supports ongoing progress.

A routine helps to build healthy habits and ensures that important aspects of recovery are consistently addressed. It provides a framework for daily activities, reducing stress and promoting a sense of control. By incorporating positive routines, recovery becomes more sustainable and effective.

The value of routine lies in its ability to create stability and support. It fosters a sense of normalcy and helps to maintain focus on recovery goals, contributing to long-term success.

November 29
Reflecting on Growth

Reflecting on personal growth involves looking back on the journey of recovery and acknowledging the progress made. It's about recognizing changes in mindset, behavior, and overall well-being and understanding their significance.

Growth in recovery often happens gradually and may not always be immediately apparent. Reflecting on this growth helps to appreciate the journey and reinforces the commitment to continued progress. It provides a perspective on how far one has come and the strength that has been developed.

Reflecting on growth enhances self-awareness and provides motivation for ongoing recovery. It turns the process into a series of meaningful achievements, contributing to a sense of accomplishment and purpose.

November 30
Preparing for the Future

Preparing for the future involves setting intentions and goals that align with the progress made in recovery. It's about looking ahead with hope and planning for continued growth and well-being. Preparation helps to create a clear path forward and reinforces the commitment to recovery.

Setting realistic and meaningful goals provides direction and purpose. It's important to envision the future with optimism and a sense of possibility, taking into account the lessons learned and the progress achieved. Preparation for the future transforms recovery from a current endeavor into a lifelong journey.

Preparing for the future ensures that the progress made in recovery is sustained and built upon. It provides a roadmap for continued growth and reinforces the commitment to living a fulfilling and purposeful life.

DECEMBER

December 1
The Gift of Awareness

Awareness is a precious gift that enhances the journey of recovery. It involves being fully present in each moment, recognizing thoughts and feelings without judgment, and understanding how they influence actions. Embracing awareness helps to navigate the recovery process with greater clarity and insight.

Awareness allows for a deeper connection to one's inner self and the surrounding environment. It provides the opportunity to observe patterns, identify triggers, and make conscious choices that support recovery. By cultivating awareness, the recovery journey becomes more intentional and mindful.

The gift of awareness enriches the recovery experience by fostering a greater understanding of oneself and the process. It transforms the journey into a path of conscious living, where each moment is approached with intention and insight.

December 2
Embracing Change

Change is an inevitable part of recovery, and embracing it involves accepting and adapting to new circumstances and challenges. It's about viewing change as an opportunity for growth rather than a disruption. Embracing change allows for flexibility and resilience throughout the recovery process.

Recovery often brings about significant changes in habits, relationships, and perspectives. Embracing these changes with an open mind and heart helps to integrate them into daily life. It's about finding comfort in the evolving journey and adapting positively to new realities. Embracing change transforms the recovery process into a dynamic and evolving experience. It fosters adaptability and growth, turning each change into a chance for personal development and deeper understanding.

December 3
Cultivating Gratitude

Gratitude involves recognizing and appreciating the positive aspects of life, even amidst challenges. Cultivating gratitude in recovery helps to shift focus from difficulties to the blessings and achievements, fostering a more positive and hopeful outlook.

Expressing gratitude for small victories, supportive relationships, and personal growth enriches the recovery journey. It creates a sense of abundance and satisfaction, highlighting the progress made and the resources available. By practicing gratitude, the experience of recovery becomes more fulfilling and hopeful.

Cultivating gratitude enhances the recovery process by reinforcing a positive mindset and appreciating the journey. It transforms the experience into one of abundance and contentment, fostering resilience and joy.

December 4
The Power of Forgiveness

Forgiveness is a powerful tool in recovery, allowing for the release of past grievances and the healing of emotional wounds. It involves letting go of resentment and embracing compassion, both towards oneself and others. The power of forgiveness fosters inner peace and facilitates emotional healing.

Forgiveness does not mean forgetting or condoning past actions, but rather releasing the hold they have on one's present well-being. It's about freeing oneself from the burden of anger and hurt, creating space for healing and growth. Forgiveness supports the journey of recovery by promoting emotional release and renewal.

The power of forgiveness transforms the recovery process by encouraging emotional healing and personal growth. It allows for a more peaceful and balanced state of mind, facilitating progress and well-being.

December 5
Building Resilient Relationships

Building resilient relationships involves creating connections that are supportive, understanding, and enduring. In recovery, resilient relationships provide a foundation of encouragement and strength, helping to navigate challenges and celebrate successes.

Resilient relationships are characterized by mutual respect, open communication, and shared goals. They offer a safe space for expressing emotions, seeking support, and working through difficulties. By nurturing these relationships, one can enhance the recovery journey and build a strong support network.

Building resilient relationships enriches the recovery experience by providing a stable and supportive foundation. It fosters a sense of belonging and strengthens the capacity to face challenges together.

December 6
Reflecting on Personal Values

Reflecting on personal values involves examining what truly matters and aligning actions with those values. In recovery, understanding and living according to personal values provides a sense of purpose and direction, guiding decisions and behaviors.

Personal values serve as a compass for navigating the recovery journey. They help to identify meaningful goals, prioritize actions, and make choices that align with one's true self. Reflecting on values ensures that the recovery process is not only about overcoming challenges but also about living a fulfilling and purposeful life.

Reflecting on personal values deepens the recovery experience by providing clarity and direction. It transforms the journey into one of intentional living, where actions and decisions are guided by core beliefs and aspirations.

December 7
The Journey of Self-Acceptance

Self-acceptance is about embracing oneself with compassion and understanding, recognizing both strengths and imperfections. In recovery, self-acceptance allows for a more forgiving and nurturing approach to personal growth and healing.

Accepting oneself means acknowledging that everyone has a unique journey and making peace with one's own path. It involves letting go of self-criticism and embracing the person one is becoming. Self-acceptance supports recovery by fostering a positive and nurturing self-image.

The journey of self-acceptance enriches recovery by promoting self-love and compassion. It transforms the process into one of personal growth and self-discovery, where acceptance becomes a foundation for healing and well-being.

December 8
Fostering a Growth Mindset

A growth mindset involves viewing challenges and setbacks as opportunities for learning and improvement. In recovery, fostering a growth mindset encourages resilience and adaptability, turning obstacles into valuable lessons.

Embracing a growth mindset involves recognizing that abilities and outcomes can improve with effort and perseverance. It's about seeing difficulties as chances to develop new skills and insights, rather than as failures. This mindset supports ongoing progress and motivates continued effort.

Fostering a growth mindset enhances the recovery journey by promoting a positive and proactive approach to challenges. It transforms obstacles into opportunities for growth, reinforcing the commitment to recovery and personal development.

December 9
The Importance of Balance

Balance is crucial in recovery, involving the harmonious integration of various aspects of life, including work, relationships, and self-care. Maintaining balance helps to prevent burnout and ensures that all areas of life are nurtured and supported.

Achieving balance involves setting boundaries, prioritizing self-care, and managing responsibilities in a way that promotes overall well-being. It's about finding equilibrium between effort and relaxation, achievement and rest, to create a sustainable and fulfilling recovery journey.

The importance of balance in recovery lies in its ability to foster a well-rounded and healthy lifestyle. It transforms the journey into one of comprehensive well-being, where all aspects of life are given attention and care.

December 10
Embracing Authenticity

Authenticity involves being true to oneself and expressing one's genuine thoughts and feelings. In recovery, embracing authenticity allows for a more honest and fulfilling experience, where actions and relationships are aligned with one's true self.

Being authentic means letting go of pretenses and living in accordance with one's values and beliefs. It involves expressing oneself openly and honestly, which fosters deeper connections and a more genuine recovery experience. Embracing authenticity supports personal growth and emotional well-being.

Embracing authenticity enriches the recovery journey by creating a more honest and fulfilling experience. It transforms the process into one of self-discovery and true connection, where being oneself is celebrated and valued.

December 11
Cultivating Patience

Cultivating patience involves accepting that recovery is a gradual process, requiring time and persistence. It's about understanding that progress may be slow and allowing oneself to move forward at a manageable pace. Patience fosters a more compassionate and realistic approach to the journey.

Patience helps to reduce frustration and stress, creating a more peaceful and accepting mindset. It involves recognizing that each step forward, no matter how small, contributes to the overall progress. Cultivating patience supports sustained effort and long-term success.

The cultivation of patience transforms recovery into a more manageable and fulfilling journey. It encourages perseverance and resilience, making the process more aligned with personal growth and acceptance.

December 12
Finding Comfort in Routine

Routine provides a sense of structure and stability, which can be comforting during recovery. Establishing a daily routine helps to create a sense of normalcy and predictability, supporting a balanced and consistent approach to the journey.

A comforting routine includes practices and habits that promote well-being and recovery. It provides a framework for managing daily activities and responsibilities, reducing stress and creating a sense of control. Finding comfort in routine helps to maintain focus and commitment.

Finding comfort in routine enriches the recovery experience by providing stability and support. It transforms the journey into a more structured and manageable process, where daily practices contribute to overall well-being and progress.

December 13
Embracing Flexibility

Flexibility involves adapting to changing circumstances and being open to new possibilities. In recovery, embracing flexibility allows for a more adaptable approach to challenges and changes, supporting continued progress and resilience.

Being flexible means adjusting plans and expectations in response to new insights and experiences. It involves letting go of rigid expectations and being open to different paths and solutions. Embracing flexibility fosters a more dynamic and responsive recovery process.

Embracing flexibility enhances the recovery journey by promoting adaptability and resilience. It transforms challenges into opportunities for growth, supporting a more fluid and responsive approach to recovery.

December 14
The Role of Reflection

Reflection plays a crucial role in understanding and integrating the recovery experience. It involves looking back on experiences, identifying patterns, and applying insights to future actions. Reflection provides clarity and perspective, enriching the journey of recovery.

Through reflection, one gains a deeper understanding of personal growth and challenges. It involves considering how past experiences influence current behaviors and decisions, and using this understanding to make informed choices. Reflection supports ongoing development and learning.

The role of reflection in recovery is to enhance self-awareness and insight. It transforms past experiences into valuable lessons, guiding future actions and reinforcing the commitment to personal growth and well-being.

December 15
Celebrating Personal Strengths

Celebrating personal strengths is an important aspect of the recovery process. It involves recognizing the unique qualities and abilities that have supported the journey thus far, acknowledging resilience, determination, and growth.

Focusing on strengths helps to build confidence and reinforces the belief in one's ability to continue progressing. It's about honoring the inner resources that have been cultivated through experience, and how they have contributed to personal transformation. By celebrating these strengths, the recovery process becomes more empowered and affirming.

Celebrating personal strengths adds a sense of accomplishment to recovery. It serves as a reminder of the progress already made and fuels further growth, encouraging a positive and self-assured mindset.

December 16
Practicing Compassion

Compassion is a key element in recovery, both towards oneself and others. It involves offering kindness and understanding, especially in moments of struggle or challenge. Practicing compassion promotes emotional healing and strengthens the connection to the recovery journey.

By showing compassion to oneself, mistakes and setbacks are approached with understanding rather than judgment. It creates an environment of self-love and acceptance, where growth is nurtured rather than stifled by harsh criticism. Offering compassion to others also fosters deeper connections and mutual support.

Practicing compassion enriches the recovery process by creating a foundation of empathy and kindness. It transforms difficult moments into opportunities for healing, promoting a gentle and supportive approach to personal growth.

December 17
The Importance of Setting Boundaries

Setting boundaries is essential for maintaining emotional well-being and personal growth in recovery. It involves clearly defining personal limits and needs, ensuring that interactions and behaviors align with what is supportive and healthy.

Healthy boundaries protect one's mental and emotional space, allowing for the focus to remain on recovery without being overwhelmed by external pressures. Establishing boundaries with others also fosters respectful and balanced relationships, where both parties understand each other's limits and needs.

The importance of setting boundaries in recovery cannot be understated, as it creates a protective and nurturing environment for healing. It transforms interactions and daily life into spaces where personal well-being is prioritized and safeguarded.

December 18

Facing Fears with Courage

Facing fears with courage is a vital part of recovery. It involves acknowledging the fears that arise along the way and taking proactive steps to confront them. Courage is not the absence of fear but the decision to move forward despite it.

Every step taken in the face of fear is a demonstration of inner strength and determination. Facing fears head-on allows for personal growth and the opportunity to overcome limiting beliefs and patterns. It's about choosing to trust in one's ability to navigate challenges.

Facing fears with courage transforms the recovery process into a path of empowerment. It fosters resilience and confidence, reinforcing the belief that no obstacle is too great to overcome with determination and perseverance.

December 19
Embracing Vulnerability

Vulnerability is often viewed as a weakness, but in recovery, it is a source of strength. Embracing vulnerability involves being open and honest about struggles, emotions, and needs, allowing for deeper healing and connection.

Allowing oneself to be vulnerable creates the space for authentic growth and support. It fosters honesty, both with oneself and others, and opens the door to meaningful relationships and interactions. Vulnerability strengthens the recovery process by promoting genuine emotional expression and release.

Embracing vulnerability transforms the recovery experience by creating a more honest and supportive journey. It fosters deeper connections with others and oneself, turning openness into a powerful tool for growth and healing.

December 20
Navigating Setbacks

Setbacks are an inevitable part of recovery, but how they are navigated determines their impact. Instead of viewing setbacks as failures, they can be seen as opportunities for learning and growth. Navigating setbacks with resilience fosters ongoing progress.

A setback does not define the overall journey but rather provides a moment to pause, reflect, and readjust. It's about understanding that recovery is not linear, and that each obstacle offers valuable insights. By approaching setbacks with patience and understanding, the journey remains on course.

Navigating setbacks with resilience transforms recovery into a more adaptable and forgiving process. It allows for continued growth and progress, turning challenges into stepping stones rather than barriers.

December 21

The Healing Power of Acceptance

Acceptance is a healing force in recovery, allowing for peace with what cannot be changed and focus on what can. It involves letting go of resistance to reality and embracing the present moment as it is, creating space for healing and growth.

Acceptance fosters inner calm and clarity, as it removes the struggle against circumstances beyond one's control. It is not about giving up, but rather finding peace in the process, even when it is difficult. Through acceptance, the path of recovery becomes more fluid and less burdened by frustration.

The healing power of acceptance transforms recovery by promoting a sense of calm and contentment. It allows for progress without the weight of resistance, fostering a deeper connection to the present moment and the journey ahead.

December 22
Strengthening Commitment

Commitment to recovery is a daily practice, one that requires reinforcement and dedication. Strengthening commitment involves actively choosing to prioritize well-being and growth, even in the face of challenges and distractions.

Commitment is about staying true to the goals set at the beginning of the journey, while also being flexible enough to adapt when necessary. It's a conscious decision to continue moving forward, even when the path feels uncertain. Strengthening commitment builds resilience and reinforces the importance of the recovery process.

Strengthening commitment in recovery transforms the journey into one of consistency and perseverance. It ensures that progress is maintained, and that the focus remains on long-term well-being and personal development.

December 23

The Role of Patience in Progress

Patience is a cornerstone of the recovery journey, as progress often unfolds gradually. It involves allowing oneself the time needed to heal and grow, without rushing or forcing the process. Patience fosters a more compassionate and realistic approach to recovery.

Progress is not always immediate or visible, but with patience, every step forward is valued. It's about trusting in the process and recognizing that meaningful change takes time. By practicing patience, the recovery journey becomes less stressful and more focused on long-term success.

The role of patience in progress transforms recovery into a more sustainable and peaceful experience. It encourages a steady and mindful approach, where each small victory is celebrated and appreciated.

December 24
The Joy of Being Present

Being present is a gift that enriches the recovery journey. It involves fully engaging with the current moment, free from distractions of the past or future. The joy of being present lies in the deep connection it fosters with oneself and the world around.

Presence allows for a deeper appreciation of life's simple moments. It brings clarity, focus, and peace to the mind, creating space for healing and growth. By cultivating presence, the recovery journey becomes a more mindful and enriching experience.

The joy of being present transforms recovery into a more fulfilling and peaceful path. It fosters a sense of gratitude and contentment, where each moment is valued for its inherent beauty and meaning.

December 25
Finding Strength in Stillness

Stillness is a powerful source of strength in recovery. It provides a space for reflection, peace, and inner calm, allowing the mind to rest and rejuvenate. Finding strength in stillness involves embracing quiet moments as opportunities for healing and insight.

Stillness fosters clarity and balance, as it creates a pause in the busyness of life. It allows for deeper self-awareness and emotional processing, creating a foundation for growth and resilience. By finding strength in stillness, recovery becomes more grounded and centered.

Finding strength in stillness transforms the recovery journey by fostering a deeper connection to oneself and the present moment. It promotes inner peace and balance, creating a more stable and resilient path forward.

December 26
Acknowledging Progress

Acknowledging progress is a vital part of recovery, as it reinforces the positive changes made along the way. It's about taking the time to recognize how far one has come, celebrating both small and large victories.

Progress is not always linear, but every step forward deserves recognition. By acknowledging progress, the recovery journey becomes more rewarding and fulfilling, motivating continued effort. It fosters a sense of accomplishment and gratitude for the growth achieved.

Acknowledging progress in recovery transforms the journey into one of celebration and positivity. It reinforces the belief in personal growth and strengthens the commitment to ongoing development.

December 27
Letting Go of Expectations

Letting go of expectations is a freeing practice in recovery. It involves releasing rigid ideas of how things should unfold, allowing for a more open and flexible approach to the journey. Letting go fosters a sense of peace and acceptance.

Expectations can create unnecessary pressure and disappointment, but by letting them go, the recovery process becomes more fluid and adaptable. It's about trusting the process without being attached to specific outcomes, creating space for growth and discovery.

Letting go of expectations transforms recovery into a more peaceful and accepting experience. It encourages openness to new possibilities, allowing the journey to unfold in its own time and way.

December 28
The Power of Intention

Intention is a guiding force in recovery, shaping actions and decisions with purpose and clarity. Setting intentions involves consciously choosing how to approach each day, aligning actions with personal values and goals.

The power of intention lies in its ability to focus attention and energy on what truly matters. It creates a sense of direction and motivation, helping to navigate the recovery process with purpose and mindfulness. By setting clear intentions, the journey becomes more intentional and meaningful.

The power of intention transforms recovery into a more purposeful and directed experience. It fosters clarity and focus, ensuring that each step forward is aligned with personal growth and well-being.

December 29
Embracing Authenticity

Embracing authenticity in recovery means allowing yourself to be fully genuine, without the need to conform to external expectations or societal pressures. Authenticity is about living in alignment with your true self—your values, emotions, and beliefs—without apology or shame.

In recovery, embracing authenticity provides a solid foundation for growth. By being true to oneself, recovery feels more aligned and personal, fostering a deeper connection to the process. Authenticity also strengthens relationships, as it promotes honesty and vulnerability in interactions with others.

Embracing authenticity transforms recovery into a journey of self-discovery and self-acceptance. It creates space for a more honest and fulfilling experience, where personal growth is celebrated in its most genuine form.

December 30
Fostering Gratitude

Gratitude is a powerful tool in recovery, as it shifts focus from what is lacking to what is present and meaningful. Fostering gratitude involves regularly reflecting on the positive aspects of life, no matter how small, and appreciating the progress made along the way.

Gratitude cultivates a mindset of abundance and contentment, which can help alleviate feelings of frustration or impatience during the recovery process. It brings attention to the supportive people, moments of joy, and personal achievements that often go unnoticed in daily life.

Fostering gratitude transforms recovery into a more joyful and fulfilling experience. It creates a sense of appreciation for the journey itself and reinforces the belief that growth is happening, even when it may not always be visible.

December 31
Embracing New Beginnings

The end of one year and the beginning of another is a symbolic time for reflection and renewal. Embracing new beginnings in recovery involves letting go of the past year's challenges and successes, while welcoming the opportunities for growth and healing that the future holds.

New beginnings offer a fresh perspective, a chance to re-commit to the recovery journey with renewed purpose and motivation. It's an opportunity to release old patterns and embrace new possibilities with openness and hope. By approaching the new year with a sense of curiosity and determination, recovery becomes a continuous process of renewal.

Embracing new beginnings transforms recovery into an ongoing journey of growth and discovery. It encourages reflection on the past, gratitude for the present, and optimism for the future, ensuring that the path forward is filled with possibility and promise.